Haunted Houses
Tales from 30 American Homes

"Matter-of-fact essays tell of eerie events . . . great ghostly fare."
  —*ALA Booklist*

"North Carolina journalist/ghost connoisseur Nancy Roberts has built a 30-year reputation researching enough hauntings to fill over 10 books, and she snares us again with these well-researched accounts."
  —*Southern Living*

"What makes Nancy Roberts' book on haunted houses of the United States so fascinating is how she has put aside all tabloid sensationalism to focus on well-researched 'substantiated' ghost stories. . . . Roberts brings credence to her stories through extensive interviews with those who have been 'haunted.' . . .
  —*Innsider*

"The author, who has been described as 'a custodian of the twilight zone,' takes the reader on a guided tour of 30 haunted houses in America. . . . Many of the places are historical landmarks open to the public and a few of them even offer overnight lodging."
  —*Away* magazine

"Roberts personally visited most of the houses featured herein: this alone sets **Haunted Houses** apart from others. . . . Tales focus upon first-hand encounters with a variety of spirits."
  —*The Bookwatch*

"All of the stories have just the right degree of scariness balanced with common sense. Delightful reading."
  —*Baton Rouge (LA) Advocate*

Haunted Houses
Tales from 30 American Homes

by **Nancy Roberts**

The Globe Pequot Press Chester, Connecticut

Library of Congress Cataloging-in-Publication Data

Roberts, Nancy.
    Haunted houses : tales from 30 American homes / by Nancy Roberts.
— 1st ed.
     p. cm.
    Includes index.
    ISBN 0-87106-775-7. ISBN 0-87106-768-4 (pbk.)
    1. Ghosts—United States. I. Title
BF1472.U6R634 1987
133.1'0973—dc 19
                                       87-20598
                                       CIP

Manufactured in the United States of America
First Edition/Fourth Printing

Contents

Preface

There are houses that you and I should, perhaps, never enter—houses that can be lived in with only the greatest understanding and tolerance.

Within them we may encounter ghostly presences, soft touches from invisible fingers, eerie sounds, the echoing footsteps of unseen inhabitants, pervasive fragrances, or even vile stenches.

There are those of us who are skeptical, but there are others who would not mind saying that, perhaps, these houses are haunted. Where are they, and what is it like to live in one of them? How do the owners adjust to curiosity seekers, to the skepticism of their friends, and, most of all, to sharing their home with an apparition?

The pages of this book contain accounts of hauntings, presences, and spectral appearances obtained from interviews conducted across the country. If you were to ask me what sort of people I talked with, I would have to describe them as ordinary people. They were down-to-earth, intelligent, and, probably, very much like yourself. In this book, I have let them tell their own unique stories.

There is often an impression perpetuated—intentionally, I believe, by so called "ghost hunters—that spirits return because of violent circumstances or for revenge. I would say this is not necessarily true and is entirely too limiting and unimaginative. As a writer who has probably researched more ghost stories based on personal interviews than any other writer, I have become convinced through conversations with those who claim supernatural encounters that there are as many reasons for the appearance of a ghost as there are kinds of people—or should I say spirits?

Nor do I believe that these presences or apparitions are necessarily tragic spirits trapped somewhere in space, unable to enter either heaven or hell. Rather, I believe that they are sometimes the recipients of an occasional and very special dispensation.

One of the most difficult decisions I have ever made in writing any book was whether to include with these accounts that of the infamous house in Amityville, New York. After visiting the town, interviewing the townspeople, and reading much of the house's abundant media coverage, including the book entitled *The Amityville Horror*, I could not suspend my disbelief long enough to write a satisfactory story in keeping with this book. Finally, my editors and I decided to omit the story, and we feel justified in doing so because of the enormous amount of material written about this house.

I have just returned from the most recent in a series of excursions that have taken me all over the United States in search of special houses with memorable ghost stories. Tonight, I sit writing by the light of a small brass-and-emerald-glass student lamp that belonged to my great-aunt. It is a reminder of the many times I lay beside her in bed at night as a child and coaxed her, "Aunt Jess, tell me a story." From her prodigious memory she would hold forth, and I was enthralled.

Not all of the narratives herein are suitable for bedtime, but that will be up to you to judge. Here is how one of the last stories I wrote for this collection begins.

"It is a summer night, and the moon is full above the Castle. That is when they say it happens, and it may be happening tonight. Pray it won't. Or pray, at least, that neither you nor I will be there to see it if it should." But wait . . . in my horror, I am getting ahead of myself. We will read later how this gruesome story begins.

There is much early history of our country in this story, and that is one of the reasons I enjoyed writing it.

On my desk is the autobiography of Jane Addams. In Chicago on a sunny day last July, I stood looking up at the second-floor windows of Hull-House. I stared as curiously as so many people have done in the past. Could I see the image of a baby, or was it only shadows on the glass? Was there ever really a baby up there like Rosemary's baby, a baby with childlike eyes that stared evilly out?

Most of the stories in this book are about places you may tour, in which you may spend the night, or which you may at least drive past and think about. (Please respect the owner's privacy when doing so.) I recall my daughter's asking once why we did not rent a house at the beach each summer, and I replied, "Honey, you have been to Cripple Creek, the Bird Cage Theater, and the office of the *Tombstone Epitaph*. You have ridden on the same dusty back road that Doc Holiday rode when he went to help Wyatt Earp shoot it out with the Clanton brothers and have visited Boot Hill where they were buried. You have gone to Acoma in New Mexico, home of the Indian tribe that vanished miraculously.

"Do you remember your visit to the famous site of the miraculous earth north of Santa Fe? You have stones from the cave of the infamous Bell Witch north of Nashville and have watched North Carolina's Brown Mountain Lights. You have visited places many people will never see!" She smiled her Mona Lisa smile and nodded.

And now, dear reader, here is your opportunity to visit some unusual and unforgettable houses!

One of the many legends that surround Old Fort Niagara, and a part of its heritage, is an old and grisly story about this building, called The French Castle. (Photo courtesy Fort Niagara.)

OLD FORT NIAGARA

Youngstown, New York

It is a summer night, and the moon is full above the Castle. That is when they say it happens, and it may be happening tonight. Pray it won't. Or pray, at least, that neither you nor I will be there to see it if it should. But wait . . . in my horror, I am getting ahead of myself. We will read later how this gruesome story began.

Old Fort Niagara at Youngstown, New York, is one of the northernmost historic sites in the United States. The impressive "French Castle," as it is called, was erected in 1726. Occupied by French voyageurs, British grenadiers, and American soldiers, these fortifications that guarded the vital water route to the West have been preserved. Here may be seen the Castle as it stood before the Revolution—the massive stone walls and bastions, blockhouses and stockade, moat and drawbridge. In the summer months the roar of muskets and roll of drums reverberate as colorful pageantry beside Lake Ontario celebrates the history of the old fortifications.

But most military forts have seen both good and evil days. Just as the body of a murdered man sometimes rises to the surface of the water to expose his murderer, dark deeds that once took place here persist among the legends surrounding Old Fort Niagara. And one grisly event continues to be told.

Our story begins in the days just before the Indian War when two soldiers, whom we shall call Henry Le Clerc and Jean-Claude de Rochefort, were stationed here. The fort in which they lived was a little city in itself, the largest place south of Montreal or west of Albany. Everything the soldiers needed for daily life was here. They had a mess hall, barracks, bakery, blacksmith shop, and, for worship, a small chapel with a large, ancient dial over the door to mark the hourly course of the sun.

The well in the center of the Castle was there in the event the fort was ever surrounded and besieged; but after the British captured it in 1759, they feared the French might have poisoned the water. Thus

1

they filled the well with dirt and covered the top with large, flat stones that matched the rest of the floor. In the 1920s, the well was restored.

In those early years a burying ground lay just outside the massive gates, and over its entrance was painted in large characters the word *rest*. How some of the poor mortals were sent to their "rest" in this barren field is open to speculation. Undoubtedly, there were those who came straight from the dungeon to the burying ground, for there is much about this fort to establish that it also served as a harsh prison.

The dungeon was called the "Black Hole," and it was a strongly built, dark, and dismal place. Over in one corner was a barbarous apparatus used for strangling poor wretches who offended the despotic rulers of those days, when both justice and mercy were in short supply. On the dungeon's walls, from top to bottom, the men who had been imprisoned here had painfully and laboriously carved their names. Sometimes, there might be a few pitiful words or a family emblem.

Imagine the distress of a merchant here at the fort who decided to hide some valuables in this dungeon when an attack was expected by a superior British force. He went there late one night and, by the light of his lantern, began to read some of the names on the dungeon wall. Among hundreds of French names, one leaped out at him. It was his own family name, d'Artagnan, carved in large letters.

To confirm the suspicions of others living near the fort that it was all too often the scene of guilt and foul murder, the bones of a woman were found when it became necessary to clear out an old sink attached to the mess hall.

Now that we know that, amidst the natural beauty of the land and the lake, there were also despotism, violence, and the most atrocious crimes, let us return to our story.

During any occupation, there is a need for celebrations to break the monotony, and the French often held parties on the third floor of the Castle. It was the custom of the officers to invite a number of Indian maidens from the nearby Seneca village to be their guests. The Seneca were one of five Iroquois tribes that occupied upper New York State, and their women had considerable power and respect. They both nominated members of the tribal council and removed them if they misbehaved.

Henri Le Clerc, a young man of a good family from Bordeaux, France, had left early on the evening of the party with several fellow officers to escort the girls to the Castle. Henri had personal reasons for going, as his heart had been captured by a lovely Indian girl named Onita. They had no sooner arrived at the village, however, than a cloudburst occurred, and no one wanted to leave until it was over. On the return to the Castle, the sky was clear and the night was beautiful, complete with an enormous full moon. Henri and Onita lingered a little behind the others admiring the moon and happy to be with each other. By the time the maidens and their escorts reached the Castle, the wine was flowing freely, for Henri could hear loud talk and outbursts of laughter as they mounted the stairs to the third floor.

"The party is already quite noisy," remarked Onita, and Henri nodded.

"If some of the men begin to get out of hand, I'll take you back to the village early," he said.

When the girls entered the room, cheers rang out; for a time there was singing and dancing, and all went well. Unfortunately, an officer named Jean-Claude de Rochefort, whom Henri particularly despised, had pulled up a chair and seated himself on the other side of Onita. Jean was a former seaman, and if he had not once been a pirate, Henri was certain he was at least a scoundrel. He also fancied himself irresistible to the ladies. All efforts that Henri and Onita made at conversation were futile, for Jean constantly interrupted; and with more wine, his behavior worsened.

Several times the girl had shaken de Rochefort's hand from her arm, but he continued to become bolder. "Mon petit chou, why do you resist me?" he said, placing his arm around her shoulders and attempting to pull her close.

"Because you are a pig!" the angry young woman shot back at him.

"Why, you little . . .," shouted Jean, seizing the girl roughly and thrusting his face close to hers.

Henri jumped from his chair and struck Jean's face such a blow that the latter released the girl in surprise. For a moment or so there was the thud of fists striking flesh and bone, and Jean was getting much the worst of it. He leaped behind a chair and, to the officers' surprise, drew his sword. Henri, who had sprung after him, now had to retreat sufficiently to draw his own weapon, and those seconds gave Jean a brief advantage.

Henri thrust repeatedly at Jean, and the greater amount of wine that the latter had consumed was now giving Henri the advantage. The blade of Henri's sword nicked Jean's arm, then his cheek. Several of the other officers at first tried to stop them but then assumed that, when one or the other was wounded, the duel would end. Jean was always volatile. His temper, combined with alcohol and the insult to his pride, sent him into a frenzy. Henri had the greater skill and ability to outlast his foe, however, and the other officers knew it. He withstood the mighty, slashing blows that deflected his skillful thrusts and avoided return lunges by stepping skillfully from one side to another to tire his enemy.

Henri moved to keep from backing into one of the Indian girls, and then he realized his danger. He was directly in front of the stairway. Seizing his advantage, Jean lunged forward with a quick thrust to the body, and involuntarily Henri stepped back to the brink of the stairway. Now Henri's peril was great, and Jean became even more reckless. He took a cut across the chin but, despite the wound, charged forward with his body like a bull, as if to grab Henri about the waist and hurl him down the stairs. Jean was a brute of a man, and to avoid grappling with him, Henri, of necessity, moved backward down the stairs.

His only hope was to keep Jean at a safe distance with the rapier-sharp point of his sword and try for a mortal thrust to the fellow's heart or abdomen. To this end, he slowly retreated down the stairs, waiting for the right moment to deliver the blow. As it seemed that the duel would be a long one, the other officers stayed on the third floor with the Indian girls. The duelists continued down the flights of steps until they were but a short distance from the first floor. Henri then began to formulate a more charitable plan: Being the more agile man, he would, when both reached the first floor, whirl around, mount a few steps, and then leap upon Jean, pinning him to the floor. If he could execute the move quickly enough, he was sure Jean would admit defeat.

But as Henri's foot reached the third step from the bottom, he tripped and lost his balance. His head struck the stone floor, and all went black. In a moment of insane anger, Jean raised his sword arm and ran the man through as he lay helpless and unconscious on the floor.

A little sanity, or at least the need for self-preservation, began to return to Jean-Claude de Rochefort. He had committed murder, a deed for which he could very likely hang. Before his crime was discovered, therefore, he must somehow get rid of the body. Henri was by no means a small man and would be too heavy to carry. Besides, Jean had only a short time to dispose of the evidence. What was he to do? He decided to dismember the body and throw the pieces into Lake Ontario. If they were found later, everyone would think that a soldier had been the victim of hostile Indians.

He began his grisly work. Using his already bloodied sword, he first cut off the head and ran with it out to the lake. Returning, he noticed the blood he had left on the floor and, finding some rags, mopped it up quickly. Ready to resume his horrible task, he heard the sound of voices from above and realized that the party was ending and that the officers and girls would be coming down the stairs at any moment. There was only one thing to do. With all his strength, de Rochefort carried the body to the well and threw it in. From the depths of the well came a distant splash, and it was done.

The partygoers stumbled back to their barracks in a much more drunken condition than the one in which they had arrived. If there were any who wondered about Henri and Jean, they probably thought both men had retired to their own quarters. Within the week some of the officers noticed the absence of Henri, and a search was organized, but it was fruitless. There were those, including the Indian girl, who were convinced that Henri had been murdered by de Rochefort, but they lacked evidence with which to step forward and accuse him.

Onita was certain that Henri was dead, for she knew he would have come back to her if he had been alive. Several months passed, and she did not have the heart to go to any parties at the Castle. But one September night when there was to be a party, she changed her mind. She would go, but only for the purpose of listening and learning whatever she could that might give some clue to the fate of Henri.

The girls and officers left the village together, and some were surprised to see Onita, for she had not been to the Castle since the duel. That night, the girl made it a point to mingle with as many of the officers as possible and not to become deeply involved in conversation with any one of them. Her objective was to find someone who was a friend of Henri's and who had been there the night he disappeared. The evening passed, but she was not successful. Finally, as she was preparing to leave with the other girls, a young man named Jacques came up and spoke to her admiringly.

"I remember you. You were the girl with Henri the night of the duel. I often admired you, but Henri was my dear friend, and I knew how much he cared about you. Your name was on his lips often."

"Thank you. Perhaps I shall see you again here at the Castle."

"Adieu," replied Jacques, nodding, and his face was flushed with pleasure.

Two weeks later Jacques went over to the village. It was on a night when the moon was huge and round with a cast to it, sometimes described as "blood on the moon." However often we mortals see it, there is always something ominous about a full moon that is red. He and Onita sat talking with some of the other members of the tribe, and this time it was Onita who brought the subject around to Henri.

"Onita, it is not wise for us to talk too much about it here. Let's walk over to the Castle."

The building was empty, for it was by now almost midnight, and the men were in the barracks. There on the first floor they sat down on the bottom step, and Jacques began to tell her how he had lingered after the others had left on the night of the duel.

"I don't know what I expected. Perhaps that Henri would come back, but he did not. I sat right where we are now."

"And what happened?"

"I thought I heard a noise coming from the well."

"The well over there?"

"Yes."

"What did you do?"

"Onita, I ran. That's what I did."

The Indian girl looked at him accusingly. "And later, you began to think that de Rochefort might have killed him and put his body in the well. Is that right?"

"Yes. I thought of that and also that he might not have been dead. Perhaps I could have saved his life."

They both fell silent. It was almost midnight, time to take Onita back to the village, thought Jacques.

"Hush! Do you hear something?" Onita whispered.

"Yes. Like something scraping against stone?"

"Do you know where it is coming from?"

"My God! Do you mean the well?"

"Yes." The clock struck midnight.

And then, as the pair watched horror-stricken, the fingers of a hand edged over the side of the well. Then another hand came up over the rim. Now the forearms of a man emerged in what had once been a soldier's uniform. The arms resting on the edge of the well appeared to push mightily, and as they did, the shoulders and upper portion of a man's body rose out of the well. Where the neck and head should have been, however, there was nothing at all.

Jacques and the Indian girl fled, terrified. They now knew the truth, for there was no doubt in their minds that de Rochefort had murdered Henri and dropped his headless body into the well. Nor did Jacques keep what he had seen a secret. The well was explored, the body of the dead man was found, and de Rochefort was hanged.

But those who have been there when the full moon is high over the Castle say that, exactly at midnight, the ghost of the headless Frenchman begins to claw its way slowly but surely out of the well. After resting from its efforts, the ghost of Henri LeClerc rises, dripping from the well, and moves slowly and awkwardly through the dark halls of the Castle in search of its long-lost head.

Old Fort Niagara is a State Historic Site operated by the Old Fort Niagara Association, Inc., in cooperation with the New York State Office of Parks, Recreation, and Historic Preservation. The address is Old Fort Niagara, Fort Niagara State Park, Youngstown, New York 14174. Telephone: (716) 745-7611. Tours are conducted throughout the year.

THE DANIEL BENTON HOMESTEAD

Tolland, Connecticut

Not far from Hartford, Connecticut, is the town of Tolland, a typical, picture-book, rural New England village. Daily life centers around the village green, with its white courthouse, churches, country store, and jail. Tolland is full of charming old houses, many built in the early 1800s. One house has a hidden room and was part of the underground railway for transporting escaped slaves to freedom. Another, toured by well-known psychics, is said to have ghosts. But the villagers didn't need anyone visiting from out of town to tell them that. They have known it for years.

In the days before the Revolution, Samuel Benton was the most prominent citizen of the area. He was from a family of shipowners, and it was rightly said in New England that all roads led eventually to the sea or, if not the sea, to the Connecticut River. The Bentons were from a port town called Wethersfield. Like Windsor and Hartford, it was a thriving port where raw materials were brought in from the southern colonies and the Caribbean. Samuel Benton's son Daniel moved from Wethersfield to the small farm community of Tolland in 1720; by then he was a well-off young man able to buy considerable acreage and build a comfortable home.

Daniel Benton and his wife lived contentedly with their children and their children's children. Of their three sons, his favorite was Elisha. The boy grew up helping with farm chores and watching the blacksmith, the tanner, and the village's various craftsmen. In his late teens he also began to watch a vivacious brown-haired girl named Jemima Barrows, the daughter of the village cabinetmaker. And if there was a sketch of some piece of furniture to be shown to Mrs. Benton for approval, Jemima was only too happy to take it to the Benton Homestead on Metcalf Road. Often, she would linger under the big sycamore tree beside the house and talk with Elisha before returning to her father's shop.

The Daniel Benton Homestead at Tolland, Connecticut, where the ghost of a Colonial Soldier has been reported. Visitors who have toured or stayed in the house also report rappings, vibrations, voices, and sobbing. (Photo by David Garrity.)

Over a year passed in this manner until, one day, Elisha asked her to marry him. Although the Bentons did not approve of the marriage, the young couple hoped time would soften their attitude. Meanwhile, Elisha and the other two sons enlisted in the Revolutionary Army.

Elisha and Jemima said their good-byes out under the sycamore tree where they had once courted. Jemima could not keep herself from envisioning her sweetheart shot by a British soldier or lying dead in the snow after some bloody battle. Her face was sad, and their wedding seemed far off as she bade him good-bye. Even as he exhorted her not to be gloomy, his own heart was heavy with foreboding.

After surrendering at the Battle of Saratoga, twenty-eight Hessian officers hired by the British to fight the colonists were housed in the stone-floored cellar of the Benton Homestead. The cellar was reasonably comfortable and had a large stone fireplace with a bake oven. The second year after Elisha's departure, a letter with a seal arrived for the Bentons, brought by a peddler. It was dated two months before and bore news from a Tolland man that two of Daniel's three sons had died while imprisoned by the British. There was no news of his favorite son, Elisha. Old Daniel died in 1776 without knowing whether Elisha was alive or dead.

One cold, windy winter afternoon, when Jemima had gone by the Benton Homestead to see if they had received any word from Elisha, there came a knock at the front door. Both women went to the door. When Mrs. Benton opened it there stood a thin, ragged, bare-footed soldier. It was Elisha. His mother and Jemima embraced him joyously, but they were bewildered by his behavior, for he kept trying to push them away.

"Don't touch me!"

"Elisha, just let us hug you. We're so glad you're safely home. You can clean up in a few minutes." And what a pathetic sight he was, but there was worse to come.

"Please, stop, both of you!"

"What is the matter, Elisha?" cried out Jemima.

"Jemima, I've come from a British pest ship in New York harbor. Most of our men on it have the smallpox!"

"But there are no marks on you," said his mother.

"I have been with men who have it."

"You are not going to get it!" said Jemima.

"I already have the chills, and my head feels as if it is splitting, it aches so," said Elisha.

"That could well be something else," said his mother. "You must bathe and then rest in your room."

"I will bathe, and while I am doing that, you must get the 'borning' room ready, Mother."

Every household had a "borning" room, and it was where some of the happiest and some of the grimmest events of Colonial life occurred. It was where women ready to deliver were placed. But it was also the room where a member of the family suffering from some disease thought to be contagious was put to die.

"No! No!" his mother protested. "If you have it, Jemima and I will probably get it anyway."

"That is true, but my father may not."

The two women looked at each other, and then Jemima nodded. "He is right."

About dusk Jemima's brother came over, sent to see why she had not returned. Mrs. Benton went to the door and told him that Elisha had come home and that Jemima would stay with them that night. She and Jemima had already decided that she would stay, for no more tragic news could have struck. Smallpox was highly contagious and one of the most dreaded diseases. Epidemics killed many people every year. If Elisha had it, Jemima should not, could not, go home. She would endanger her entire family and probably seal their death warrant.

After a hot meal Elisha seemed to feel better, and the two women became more optimistic. Elisha's father, Daniel, went to the doorway of the room and talked with him, but he did not go in. Before the evening meal, Benton thanked God for his son's return and prayed that he might be healed, "If it be Thy will, oh, Lord."

"Why do you say that, Daniel? You know it is God's will that our Elisha be healed. God is good."

"The Lord giveth and the Lord taketh away," intoned Benton.

"Sickness taketh away, and that is none of the Lord's doing!" She flushed under her husband's disapproving look.

Jemima's eyes filled with tears. "We do not know of a certainty that he has it."

"That is right, Jemima," said Mrs. Benton.

When they all left the warmth of the hearthside for their beds, Elisha's mother and Jemima looked in on him. He was sleeping peacefully, and the flush seemed to have left his cheeks. The next day they were all much encouraged, for Elisha did not appear feverish and he ate well. Jemima sat in a chair beside his bed, and for the first time he seemed eager to talk about their plans for the future.

Her parents drove up in their carriage later that day, and Jemima talked with them but did not ask them to come in. She told them how encouraged his parents and she were about Elisha and that he must be wrong about having the disease, but Mrs. Barrows' eyes were dark with fear.

"Of course, it's best that you stay here. Not for your father's and my sake, you understand, but for your brothers and sisters. Your older brother will be over tonight and leave clean clothing for you."

Everyone was in a more cheerful frame of mind at supper, and Daniel once more sought the Lord's help, this time without qualifying his petition.

But in the early hours of the morning, Jemima awakened. She could hear Elisha groaning, and when she reached his room, his mother was already there bathing him with cloths wrung out in cool water. Elisha was suffering waves of the most terrible nausea, and his thin body was on fire with fever. By the next morning red spots had appeared on his face and arms, and later they covered his body and legs. Then the spots began to swell, and soon they filled with fluid. There was no need to call a physician. Even if one were to risk coming, there was no known cure for the disease.

Jemima and Mrs. Benton nursed and prayed, pleading for Elisha's life with a deity who thus far had not answered. If Elisha survived this stage and the blisters dried up, and that is what they were waiting and watching for, the fever would break and improvement would begin. His skin would be pockmarked for life, but at least he would be alive. When he wouldn't eat, at first they had at least been able to get him to drink soup; but by the third week, he refused even that. After taking no nourishment for two days, he died in Jemima's arms. Now her grief was inconsolable, and she lay in the room for hours, sobbing.

Not long after Elisha's death, Jemima was seized with chills. She took her sweetheart's place in the "borning" room and suffered alone. The Barrows brought food and left it at the door or window (There were no porches then.) each day. Sometimes Jemima was delirious, and, forgetting that he was dead, she would call Elisha, begging him to come to her.

Then one morning, when Mrs. Benton went to the door of Jemima's room with a bowl of broth and spoke to the girl, there was no answer. Jemima was dead. It was February 28, 1777, four weeks after her sweetheart's death.

Mrs. Yvonne Brown, a member of the Tolland Historical Society and a former chief docent for tours of the Benton house, says, "There have always been reports of ghosts in the Homestead." Whether it is the often reported ghost of a Hessian soldier or that of Elisha returning to see his sweetheart, no one can be sure.

Psychics Ed and Lorraine Warren went through the house and claimed that they saw a young girl in her teens. But some of the most interesting stories have come from the townspeople. If they prefer to remain anonymous, it is because Tolland is still a small place where people do not want to be the target of their neighbors' jokes. I would like to share some brief quotes that Yvonne Brown attributes to "down-to-earth, professional-type people."

"At one time before the Historical Society took it over, the home was rented briefly to a young married couple. The wife told me, 'I was asleep in the front bedroom when the most terrible sobbing started, and I was immobile with fear until it stopped.'"

A member of the Society related a strange experience with her dog. "The dog and I went into the summer kitchen, but she would not go into the dining room with me. I picked her up and carried her to the sitting room and walked toward the dining room, calling her to come in. She again refused to enter. I wonder what was in that dining room that bothered her so. One of the most startling experiences was one evening when the tenant had a guest. "We were sitting before the fire enjoying ourselves when our visitor asked, 'What is that?' We all listened while light footsteps tripped down the hall. There was a small thump, more light footsteps, and then all was quiet. Our visitor left within fifteen minutes."

Others speak of lights in the house that come on repeatedly right after they have turned them off and of twigs that snap in a fireplace in the summer when it is not in use, as if someone is laying a fire. And there have been those who have heard the sound of men's voices.

Recently, a newspaper reporter was being shown the house, and she asked whether the huge hearthstones had come from the property. Before the hostess had a chance to answer, three knocks were heard, as if to say, "Yes, they did." The two women looked at each other, and the reporter said she had to go.

"The most interesting tour I ever conducted of the house was on a day when it was not normally open," says Yvonne Brown. "The town clerk called to ask if I would show the Benton Homestead to a couple from Miami. The man's name was William H. Benton, III, and his wife was Pamela Jenner. The Daniel Benton Homestead was his ancestral home, and since they were visiting her brother in Connecticut, they had decided to make what they called a "commemorative visit" to the Homestead.

Benton was the direct descendant of Daniel, who had owned much of Tolland, and it was his ancestor Elisha who died of smallpox in this house. Pamela, his wife, was a direct descendant of Edward Jenner, who in 1796 (according to the Encyclopaedia Britannica, compiled and edited by William Benton) injected the first safe inoculation against smallpox.

"What an incredible chain of circumstances brought that couple to the house," says Yvonne Brown. Indeed, it would seem that coincidence can be equally as strange as ghosts.

The Daniel Benton Homestead at Tolland, Connecticut, is owned by the Tolland Historical Society, Tolland, CT 06084. Telephone: (203) 875-6638. It is open to the public for tours on Sunday afternoons, 1-4 PM, from May through October.

SEVEN STARS TAVERN

Woodstown, New Jersey

There are houses that exude an overwhelming sense of mystery, houses that seem to reach out and capture your imagination by evoking thoughts of the specters and ghosts of people who have lived within them. For me, there was just such a house.

Years ago, when I was a child living in Woodstown, New Jersey, I would pass the house on sunny days and sometimes during a rainstorm, or I would see it looming up darkly beside the road, shrouded by the dense fog common to this low-lying area. But whatever the weather, I invariably felt the house's spell. It is named the Seven Stars Tavern, and it was built in 1762 at the intersection of Kings Highway and the Woodstown-Auburn Road.

As I researched this book, one of the places that I thought would have some good ghost stories was the South Jersey area around Woodstown and Salem, towns only a few miles apart. I questioned the librarian at the Salem Library about any houses with ghost stories surrounding them.

"Seven Stars Tavern is the one I think of first," she replied. "In fact, the head of the Camden Historical Society at one time called it the most haunted house in New Jersey." I was taken aback, for the sense of mystery I had felt so often about this house was now confirmed. My perceptions of something supernatural being there had been correct, although at that time I had only a casual interest in ghost stories. Yet the house, which is an impressive and beautiful place, does not remotely resemble most people's mental picture of a haunted house.

When I contacted Robert and Marjorie Brooks, the people who now live in this historic building, a second surprise awaited me: Marjorie and I had attended school together in Woodstown when she was Marjorie Robbins. Her relatives owned the tavern for most of the

Seven Stars Tavern, near Woodstown, built in 1762, is said to be the "champion haunted house of New Jersey." A group of farm workers who stayed there in the thirties found this out, to their horror. (Photo by Mary Waddington Smith.)

nineteenth century. The original owners, Peter and Elizabeth Louderback, ran a tavern for travelers. They changed their name from Lauterbach to Louderback, the way Americans pronounced it, and, according to Robert Brooks, it was rumored that the Louderbacks buried their valuables somewhere on the property to hide them from British soldiers during the Revolution. Peter's apparition is said to return to the tavern in search of his treasure.

There are many stories of the supernatural connected with Seven Stars, but space here allows for only the most famous one. It is the somewhat gory story of the ghost of the Tory Spy. The event upon which the story is based is said to be a historical fact. According to Brooks, the story goes that a man loyal to the British during the Revolutionary War was supplying information to King George's soldiers. The soldiers would then conduct foraging raids, stealing cows and food from area farmers. Neighbors found out about the Tory's actions and decided to take care of the scoundrel. A group of men dragged him up to the attic of Seven Stars, tied one end of a rope around his neck and the other around a wooden beam, and tossed him out the window.

In the 1930s there was a man living in the Salem area named John Klein. He was one of four harvesters employed to cut the grain for the Robbins family, who owned Seven Stars Tavern. Nathaniel ("Natty") Robbins always had difficulty getting help locally because the house had a reputation for being haunted. Finally, Natty was fortunate enough to hire John Klein, who had no fear of ghosts, and three workers named Simon, Sam, and Jim, who were just passing through.

It was the custom for farm hands to sleep in the large attic of the house, which was furnished only with some chairs, a bowl and pitcher on top of an old pine washstand, and straw mattresses on the floor. After their first day's work, the four men were too tired to notice the musty smell of old wood and moldy straw. That night, all went to bed early, and their sleep was deep.

The second day Simon went about his work with a glum silence that irritated his friend and companion, Sam. All four men worked hard and retired early that night, again from exhaustion; but before extinguishing the lamp, Simon asked if anyone had heard anything strange the night before. His two friends at once connected this with his long face that day and assured him that he must have been dreaming. This is what he wanted to believe, but Simon was still uneasy, for he could not rid himself of the certainty that he had not been dreaming. It was far too vivid.

Simon knew that, if he said more, he would be ridiculed; as it was, his friends made jokes about his drinking too much of Natty's cider. But the next day Simon's spirits were still melancholy. He avoided his friends entirely, and just before dark, he made some pretext to slip away and climb up to the attic alone. When the others came up laughing and talking, they found Simon up in the rafters that supported the roof—marking crosses on the timbers with a piece of chalk. They joked about his "getting religion" so suddenly, but he said nothing, and as soon as he had swung himself down, he blew out his candle and turned in.

Something awakened Sam during the night, and to his astonishment he saw Simon seated on a chair, staring straight ahead and rigid as a post. At his feet were two lighted candles. The agony of fear on Simon's face was real.

"What's wrong?" asked Sam, springing to his feet.

"Shhh!" whispered Simon, holding up a hand to quiet him. His face was white and his eyes were wide as he gazed in the direction of the stairway. Sam roused the two other men as quietly as possible, but perhaps he made more noise than he thought, for Simon repeatedly hissed "Shhh" at them and motioned agitatedly for them to be quiet. The men could not help being frightened, although they had no idea what had happened. There was a terrifying sense of some imminent peril.

In profound silence they sat and waited. Finally, John Klein whispered, "What is it, Simon?"

"Shhh! Ghosts!" Simon whispered back. "I heard 'em again. They may come back up here. They're downstairs."

John Klein was not afraid of ghosts, but what Simon whispered shook his confidence temporarily. Yet it was not what Simon had said or even the conviction with which he had said it that upset Klein as much as the fact that, now and then, he would whisper a few stuttering words and then give a startled jump. The story, as Klein was able to put it together, was that he had actually heard the ghosts the previous night when the men said he had only been dreaming. At first, Simon said, the ghosts were far away. Then they came nearer. Finally, there had been a terrible scuffle on the stairway with much shouting and swearing. Then a group of brawling spirits had come thronging up the ladder into the attic and headed for the window near Simon's mattress. "They pushed and shoved right up to my window and went out through it as if they were smoke! Twice now, I've seen them and heard them."

"How do you know they are ghosts?" asked John Klein.

"If they were human they would all be dead. That window is sixty feet above the ground, but they're not dead. I heard them clatter back in again. Shhh! They're downstairs now."

All was darkness except for the shadows of the men moving as the candles flickered. Simon made them lock the door at the foot of the stairway. John Klein and Sam did so. Next he ordered that all the attic windows be closed and wedged, too, and they did that also. In silence, they sat and waited, hearing only the beating of their own hearts. Simon would not let them set their chairs over any crack in the floor because, as he told them, "When the ghosts found the door barred they'd come up through the cracks in the floor."

Not a sound. They were all apprehensive, yet there was nothing but a prolonged stillness. After some time, Jim broke the silence and told the others they were all "blank fools" and that he was going back to bed. The rest followed sheepishly.

How long they had been asleep is uncertain, but they were brought to their feet by the most hellish screams of terror. Simon was nowhere to be seen. By the light of a candle that someone lit, they found him, almost hidden, down in the angle where the floor met the sloping roof, his face to the corner and his hands clasping his head. He was screaming and sobbing, praying and writhing, and all the time kicking as if to get away from somebody or something.

Simon's screams brought up Natty Robbins and the women. It was the women, more than the men, who finally succeeded in calming Simon down. When he was able to control himself, this is the account he gave of what had happened after the four men had gone back to bed.

I was sound asleep. I didn't hear any noise at all, but, before God, when I woke up quick, I *felt* something. I tried not to do it, but I couldn't help pulling the sheet back and peeking out. There was just nothing I could see because the candles had been blown out, and there wasn't a bit of light. I knew there was danger.

Suddenly, I heard a steady thump, thump, thump on the stairs, as if someone was striking with a light hammer, and my eyes were riveted in that direction. It was the pitch black of night, but just as plain as if he had been made of moonlight, I saw a man slowly coming up the stairs. First appeared only his head, then his body, and finally his whole figure. He held the end of a heavy rope in his two hands, with which, at each step, he hit the step ahead of him. Although he wore heavy boots, there was never a sound from them, only the thump, thump, thump of the rope end and a bubbling sound in his throat, as if he were trying to say something and couldn't.

After reaching the top of the stairs, he advanced straight toward the window by my bed. I thought if I kept still and he didn't see me, he'd go on past me and out the window as the others had done. Then I'd be well shut of him. But just before he got to my bed, he commenced a violent grabbing and tugging at his throat with his two hands. All the time he was making the most horrible choking noises and twisting his body and striking out with his boots in a way that I thought would be the end of me.

Then, all of a sudden, he quieted. He threw out his arms and raised his head as if praying, all the while moving toward the window. I had sense enough to know that he would soon be gone, and I felt easier. But when he was right opposite me, I could see that there was a rope tied tight around his neck and hanging down behind. God, how I remember the sound of that trailing rope, for I had heard it before, not knowing what it was.

My trouble had only begun, for, instead of going on past me as I had prayed he would, he suddenly halted, dropped his arms, and stood looking down at me. I tried to call the boys but was too terrified to make a sound. Then, kneeling down, the ghost threw back his head and thrust his swollen neck with the rope around it close before my face. I couldn't stir. He pointed to his throat, out of which was coming those ghastly gurgling noises, and he repeated those violent motions I had seen before. Now I saw that they were efforts to untie the rope around his neck. His face and neck were blue and swollen, and a bloody froth oozed from his lips.

He reached out and took my two hands in his, raising

them to his throat. I somehow found strength to pull them back. He gently took them again, and something made me understand that he wanted me to loosen the knot. Somehow, I did it. I don't know how. He leaped up, uttering the most devilish "Ha! Ha! Ha!" and disappeared through the window. And that is the last I remember until daybreak.

Simon, Jim, and Sam left the tavern the next day. John Klein worked a day or two longer and left. Not that he was afraid of ghosts, said he, but because he couldn't get Simon's screams out of his ears. As he finished telling this story to his son, he shook his head and said, "What's the use of working all day at a place where you can't get any sleep at night?"

The Tory Spy was never again seen at Seven Stars, and John Klein swore that Simon's cries scared him off, but others believe Simon laid the ghost to rest when he was brave enough to untie the knot and free him.

Said to be the best-preserved colonial tavern in the East, Seven Stars was built in 1762 by Peter and Elizabeth Lauterbach, (later Louderback) whose descendants own the Louderback North American Van Lines. For more than a decade, the tavern was the home of Roy Plunkett, inventor of Teflon. It is now the property of Robert and Marjorie Brooks of Woodstown. Though it is not open to the public, passers-by may view it at the intersection of Kings Highway and Woodstown-Auburn Road.

THE MYRTLES

St. Francisville, Louisiana

S t. Francisville, Louisiana, is a charming old town some seventy miles north of New Orleans. It is built on a narrow ridge and said to be "two miles long and two yards wide." There are many beautiful plantation homes there, but the only one with eerie happenings that have reverberated throughout America is The Myrtles.

The Myrtles is one of the haunted houses that have been featured in *Life* magazine, *Southern Living*, the *Wall Street Journal*, *USA Today*, *Family Circle*, and many other publications. In fact, the list of periodicals and television networks that have done features on this house is almost endless. The Myrtles is also, according to the United States Tourist Bureau, one of the authenticated haunted houses of America, and it has sometimes been called America's most haunted house.

The house contains some of the most interesting architecture in the South. The outside of this home, built by General David Bradford in 1796, has 240 feet of lacy, ornamental ironwork, and within, the large rooms with high ceilings are graced by outstanding plaster friezes. It is surrounded by ninety-one immense oak trees dripping with Spanish moss, and beneath them the house appears to be in perpetual twilight. "Unlike other houses, to me, The Myrtles is an entity," says its owner, Frances Kermeen.

How did a vivacious blonde from the West Coast with hazel eyes, an attractive smile, and the voice of an engaging teenager become the owner of a house like this? And what eerie experiences has she encountered? Ms. Kermeen shares her story.

"We were on a cruise to Jamaica and Haiti and then on to Acapulco. While we were on the cruise, we became friendly with another couple who talked us into skipping Acapulco and coming back to Louisiana with them. Because this is such a lovely place and, really, just for fun, we decided to look at real estate while we were here.

The Myrtles, St. Francisville, Louisiana. (Photo by Susan A. Bush.)

The day we were looking was the day the listing on The Myrtles came into the office.

"I later found out that a couple who lived directly behind my parents' house in San Jose had gone on the same cruise we had [twenty years earlier] and stopped in St. Francisville on their way back to Michigan. The house happened to be for sale at the time, and they bought it under almost identical circumstances.

"That first day in the real estate office, as we were going out to look at the house, the realtor kept calling me Sarah, although I corrected her several times. Neither of us were aware of it, but later I found that two Sarahs had lived in this house in the 1800s. When I went into the house for the first time, I heard a woman's voice calling my name. At first I thought it was the realtor, but she was outside trying the back-door key to be sure it worked. After I left, I knew I would be buying the house, and I cried some that night as I realized that from now on, I would be far from my family and home.

"As I think about everything that happened, fate, or I prefer to call it God, has played an important part in the events of my life. I also think that places exert a strong pull on certain individuals, and I will always believe that this house *chose me*.

"The first week I was there, I was sleeping in an upstairs bedroom. I left the lights on, but the switch was turned most of the way around and set on "dim." After a night or two, I thought that was silly and that I could sleep with the lights off, so I turned them off. But sometime after midnight I woke up and the lights were on bright. Half asleep, I thought I must have left them on and I turned the dial. The room was once more in darkness. Two hours passed, and I was awake again. I found all the lights in the room on bright just as they had been two hours earlier. I turned the switch 360 degrees and clicked the lights off again. It was almost daybreak when I woke up for the third time, and the lights were on once more. That just scared me to death, and I grabbed my robe and blanket to go downstairs and sleep in the sitting room.

"All went fine, and I slept peacefully until about five o'clock, when I woke up with a start and the feeling that someone was looking at me. I stared up into the face of a large black lady whose head was wrapped in a green turban. She wore something that resembled a long, green dressing gown. I was so shocked that I just couldn't look back at her face. By that time I had begun screaming, but she still didn't go away. Involuntarily, I struck out with my arm to push her from me; but as I did so, my hand passed through her, and she faded away.

"It was a couple of days before the closing on the house, and the owner was still there. I told her about it the next day, and she said, 'That's ridiculous!' Even on the first night, at about one o'clock, I had heard footsteps outside my door and assumed it was one of the other houseguests. The next day I learned that everyone in the house claimed to have been dead to the world before eleven. Later I found the whole town knew that the house was haunted, but they weren't about to tell an out-of-state person who was thinking about buying it. After I had bought the house, I mentioned the lady in green to the mother of the owner, and to my surprise, she was absolutely thrilled. Can you imagine? She said, 'Why, Frances, you have seen The Myrtles' most famous ghost!'

"I turned the house into a bed-and-breakfast place, and at first I tried to keep the ghostly visitors a secret from the real ones. But during the seven years I have been here, there have been about a hundred reports each year of apparitions or some supernatural occurrence. There were times when I was truly frightened, and the only thing that kept me from going back to my parents was that it would be too embarrassing to tell them I was leaving because I was afraid of ghosts.

"The most common sounds are either those of children's voices at play or those of a baby crying. But the eeriest of all is the music of a ball going on downstairs. Often people think that someone has their television on too loud, but then they find that there isn't even a television set in the room next to them. Each room has its own unique ghost. One has a wounded Confederate soldier who appears in it in May and June. A pair of honeymooners was here, and he went upstairs alone to lie down. He woke up to find a black servant standing beside the bed bandaging his foot. The honeymooners checked out, even though they had prepaid."

The plantation's most famous murders occurred shortly after its sale in 1817 to a philandering judge named Clarke Woodruff, General Bradford's son-in-law. The judge grew angry with a slave woman named Cleo for eavesdropping, and he cut off one of her ears as a penalty. For revenge, she mixed poisonous oleander flowers into a birthday cake for the judge's oldest daughter. His two little girls died, as had his wife. Other slaves hanged Cleo, and it is said she still haunts the house, wearing a green turban to hide the missing ear. She was evidently the ghost that frightened Frances Kermeen during the latter's first week in the house.

Janet Roberts, a psychic who is the treasurer of the Louisiana Society for Psychical Phenomena, believes that The Myrtles has many ghosts. "Walking into the parlor was like walking into a crowded cocktail party. I felt that we were literally bumping into people, and I wanted to say, 'Excuse me.' " But except for the grump who will occasionally hurl a clock or drop a candlestick, the ghosts do no harm.

Ms. Kermeen continues, "I have been in the house for seven years now and at first would not stay here alone at night. In 1981, I made it into a bed-and-breakfast place, and after that I was seldom alone here. But there are still a few things that rile me, and when they do, I have to go spend the night in the new wing."

Asked if she had ever talked with any of the apparitions, Ms. Kermeen shook her head. "I certainly am not brave enough to try and communicate with any of them. I got used to the footsteps, the door slamming, and the voices, so now I don't keep my hand on the phone, ready to dial the police as I did at first. I know this sounds absurd, but it's funny what you later come to accept when you didn't believe in this sort of thing at all before.

"About 75 percent of the people who come here do so because they want to hear about our ghosts. The other 25 percent just happen upon it. Oddly enough, the ones who get scared and want to check out in the middle of the night are sometimes the big, macho-type men."

What sort of person is most apt to have a supernatural experience? Says Ms. Kermeen, "It is usually the skeptic or the one that isn't expecting anything to happen. When people have been so eager to see a ghost and then report it, I wonder if it isn't their imagination.

"There have been ten murders here at The Myrtles, and that's quite a few, even for a house that is almost 200 years old. I think some of those poor, tragic victims may have been the ghosts I have seen. I believe this house sets off intense emotions in the people who live here for any length of time. The overseer of this plantation in 1850 was a white man twenty-four years old, and he committed suicide. I later hired a young man of twenty-four who tried the same thing. Fortunately, he was unsuccessful. He may have been unstable from the beginning, but some people are very impressionable. I don't hire men that age any more. I try to hire happy people, and I have always been a healthy, happy person myself. Most visitors who come here seem to leave content and rested. At least I think they do, for a great many return each year.

"At first the ghosts terrified me. Then there was a year or two when the knowledge that they were there was just fun and games. But of late, I really believe that they have led me to God. They have brought me closer to a sense of His reality and the meaning of life. Once you are confronted with a ghost, you can't brush off the existence of life after death."

———————————

For more information, write The Myrtles Plantation, Highway 61, P.O. Box 387, St. Francisville, Louisiana 70775 or telephone (504) 635-6277.

WHITE OAKS

Charlotte, North Carolina

I t is hard to live in a city the size of Charlotte, North Carolina, for a quarter of a century and not hear some fascinating ghost stories. But when that city is home, you know the family connections, and you are aware that others do, too. Will they recognize someone or even themselves, and how much personal embarrassment will a story cause?

Keeping to the facts, but with some disguising of names, we will take that risk and relate a story of more than usual interest to those of us interested in the supernatural. Since I was for several years a confidante of the woman in this story, I was able to keep up with the events. The woman was a writer, and her occupation caused her to meet many well-to-do Charlotteans, but it would be far better if I were to let the young woman, whom we will call Karen, tell the experience in her own words.

"I had an assignment to do a story on an historic house called White Oaks. My interview was set for late in the afternoon, and my hostess had told me there would be a party going on for a performing-arts group."

" 'Your presence won't be any inconvenience at all, Karen. In fact, why not plan to just be one of my guests and enjoy yourself,' the woman suggested graciously.

"When a story subject had to cancel, I decided to go home early and change from a tailored suit into a new, red cocktail dress that was infinitely more flattering. I remember thinking how foolish it was, but something overruled my usual practicality, and as I drove down Providence Road in all my finery, I was excited about the evening ahead.

"When I first saw the colonial mansion, I thought, Scarlett O'Hara would certainly have felt at home here. Once owned by the late James B. Duke, this stately sixty-five-year-old house in the heart of Charlotte's Eastover section is almost as tall as the branches of the

24

"White Oaks," an historic Charlotte house where a promise resulted in a startling, macabre experience.

towering trees that surround it. White Oaks, as it is called, was part of that grand scale of living to which Duke, a tobacco king, was accustomed.

"I knocked, thinking the butler would answer. Instead, the door opened almost immediately, and there stood, not the butler, but the most handsome man I had ever seen. He had dark, curly hair with a distinguished hint of gray, expressive blue-green eyes, and a dazzling smile. He pretended in a charming and amusing fashion to be the butler. We were both laughing as we walked together down the white-and-black-marble entrance hall. He introduced me to a group of other guests, who stood chatting and sampling hors d'oeuvres at one end of the room, which was the size of an elegant ballroom.

"My impromptu escort was obviously the center of the women's attention, and he had no sooner introduced himself to me as Jon than two plump ladies came up and, with an arm through each of his, carried him off. He appeared to be drifting away on a pair of water wings and looked back as if reluctant to go.

" 'Well, here you are,' said my hostess, appearing at my elbow. 'Everyone seems to be entertaining themselves. This is a good time to take you on a tour of the house. It has changed considerably since Nanaline Duke lived here, but I doubt if she would mind the changes we've made.'

" 'Oh, did the Dukes live here long?'

" 'Only about six years, and Nanaline far less than her husband or daughter. She made no bones about finding Charlotte dull; and when they visited here, she usually left before the rest of the family.'

"I gazed admiringly at the hand-carved marble fireplace at one end of the room. The gold leaf in this room was lovely. 'That was applied by the Dukes. We used masking tape to protect it while we were repainting,' my hostess said. The round, oak table looked almost lost in the oversized kitchen, and along one side wall was an immense, hooded gas range that had been used by the servants of former families.

"There were beautiful classical mantels, marble hearths, and tiles around the fireplaces. Bathroom fixtures were early ceramic castings, and there were elaborately detailed brass fixtures. Some of the lighting resembled early Colonial candles or oil lamps. In the dining room was one of the most magnificent crystal chandeliers I had ever seen.

"My hostess suddenly turned and asked, 'Have you and Jon Avery known each other long?'

" 'I met him tonight. Why do you ask?'

" 'It's just that he is married. His wife has been in a sanitorium for the last three years.'

" 'I'm sorry to hear that, but, really, that is the first conversation I have ever had with him and probably the last.' As if to make me out a liar, there was a masculine voice at my elbow, and it was Jon's.

" 'I've brought you some champagne, caviar, and a sandwich. I hope this will lure you into talking with me, Karen.'

" 'How can I resist such thoughtfulness?' I asked, genuinely hungry, and what possible harm could there be in a few minutes spent with this man? For the first time I noticed he had a slight limp. Someone was discussing track, I believe. At any rate, we both heard it, and he turned to me saying, 'I'm sure you've noticed this limp that I have. It is the result of polio when I was a child. I used to resent the fact that I came along before Dr. Salk and his sugar cubes with vaccine in them.'

" 'You met me at the door and escorted me in, and I certainly wasn't aware of it then,' I said, which was true.

This seemed to please him very much, and he went on to tell me that, through hours of exercise, he became able to play volleyball in college and since then had walked at least three miles a day. We went on to talk of current events and his hobby of photography. Thinking it over later, I knew this man was undeniably attractive. He had one of the quickest minds I have ever encountered, and I had enjoyed our talk very much, but that was where it ended.

"The next day was Friday, and I picked up the phone at my office to hear Jon Avery's voice asking if I would join him for dinner. I had plans for the evening with a new executive who had come to the paper from another city. We had lunched together several times, and it was just a friendship. I might have changed our dinner to another night if I had wished to do so. But I could not forget that warning of my hostess. I was polite, but my voice held Jon at arm's length as I told him I had other plans. That should be it.

"Less than a week had passed when I was surprised by a call from White Oaks with an invitation to return. My hostess was having a few people over for drinks, and among them were a couple who had once lived in the house. If I had not done my story, she wondered, would I enjoy talking to them? Of course, I accepted. We had been seated for less than an hour on the brick terrace surrounding the house when the doorbell rang. In a few minutes, I heard the faint sound on the terrace of someone walking with a limp. For some insane reason, I could feel my heart thud. Of course, it was Jon, and I felt that he was as surprised to see me as I to see him.

"How beautiful it was that afternoon with the blooms of dogwoods, cherry trees, and azaleas. The other guests went off to tour the house, and Jon suggested that I might like to go out and look at the gardens and fountain. "Buck" Duke had done everything well, and there was nothing like it anywhere else in Charlotte. How long we stood talking at the edge of a circular garden near the fountains, I have no idea, only that, when we came back and my hostess looked at me, I felt some guilt and embarrassment.

"I knew something had happened that evening between Jon and me, and during the coming months, it seemed to block out all possible consequences or normal feelings of guilt. When I did consider the future, it was with all sorts of romantic imaginings. His wife would probably not live long, and he was aware of it; or he would divorce her, and we would move to another city after setting up a generous trust for her lifetime care. All obstacles would somehow miraculously disappear, melted by the fervency of our love for each other.

"But in August I began to realize that Jon's sense of responsibility would never allow him to divorce his wife and anything other than marriage would be impossible for me. More and more her apparition was present when we were together, for I had begun to feel sorry for this woman I had never met. What was the answer to this painful situation? Could I dart between the horns of a dilemma and emerge unscathed? No. The only right decision was to end such a doomed romance.

"That night, as I left Queens Road and turned down Ardsley, I knew I must not weaken. Jon had arrived first. There was a large party going on at White Oaks, and just as we had on that fateful evening in the early spring, we walked again in the garden. Everything about Jon's manner—the tension, the pleading expression in his eyes—told me he sensed what I planned to tell him. After I told him what I must do, we were both in agony and stood silently together near the fountain. What could be said to assuage such hurt?

" 'I must go now. I really must.' I looked at my watch, and it was midnight.

" 'Karen, do just one thing for me, please. It is all I shall ever ask of you on this earth.'

" 'What is it?'

" 'I will agree to all you have said. Just promise to meet me here one year from tonight at the same hour.'

"I was reluctant at first, thinking of how difficult it would be to see him and how bad it would be for us both, as it would only reopen partially healed wounds. But at last I consented.

" 'Well, I will come if I am alive.'

"He grasped me by the wrist. 'Don't say that, Karen. Say alive or dead!'

" 'All right, then. We will meet, dead or alive.' Thus, we parted.

"The next year I was on the spot a few minutes before the appointed time, and Jon arrived punctually at midnight. I had begun to regret the arrangement I had made, but it was a promise. Although I kept the appointment, I said that I really did not wish to do so again. Jon, however, persuaded me to renew it for just one more year, and I consented, although much against my better judgment. We again said our good-byes, repeating the promise, 'Dead or alive.'

"I had begun to see a delightful man, and late the following spring we became engaged. The summer was spent boating on Lake Norman, with occasional trips to visit Alex's family in the North Carolina mountains at Montreat. They were prominent Presbyterians, his father active and respected in the denomination. On their return from Montreat in August, we were planning a September wedding and a honeymoon that would begin on Labor Day weekend.

"By early July, I had begun to think more and more about my promise to Jon. The last thing I wanted to do was to meet him in the garden again. The days sped past with terrible swiftness, and the thought of that meeting hung over me like a dark cloud. I didn't want to go. I didn't want to go at all. But I had promised. I supposed the only thing that could get me out of it was death. Not even that, really, for I had promised to go dead or alive. Dead or alive! What a macabre promise to ask of me.

"How would Alex feel about my meeting another man in a secluded place at midnight? I knew very well that he wouldn't like it. Should I talk to him with the hope he would understand? Was he likely to understand my dating a married man, even one married to an invalid in a sanitorium? Guilt overwhelmed me.

"As the last Monday night in July approached, I became more and more apprehensive. If I were to find out about Alex meeting a woman under such peculiar circumstances a short time before our wedding, I would consider calling the wedding off. Would he feel that way if he found out? Finally, I decided I would confide in my long-standing friend and apartment-mate and ask her to accompany me. Sherry said she would go to be sure I was all right.

"That night I arrived at the garden about ten minutes before twelve, thinking I would leave, having kept my promise, if he were not there by midnight. The area near the brick terrace was empty, and I did not see a soul. But at five minutes before twelve, I heard a slight sound. Then it came again. Finally, ever so softly, the sound became constant. It was the sound of footsteps on the brick terrace, but the footsteps were slower than normal and had just the slightest dragging sound. It is he, I thought, for I had heard that walk too often to mistake it. Tonight he was right on time.

"I knew that what I must tell him about my approaching marriage would hurt, even though he had surely resigned himself to the end of our romance. The footsteps were coming closer. Soon I would have to break the news about Alex. Sherry was at a discreet distance but close enough to see me standing by the fountain in the brilliant moonlight. On came the footsteps. Why so slow? Why was it taking him so long?

"I was not only ashamed to be there but angry that I had allowed myself to be persuaded to come a second time. This would be our last meeting, for I would not stay. I could see him now and watched him make his way into the moonlight at the end of the terrace. On he came past a large azalea and along the drive. It would all be over soon, thank heaven.

"When he was close enough for me to see him more clearly, I noticed that he was dressed in dark, formal attire. He must be doing this for its effect on me, I reasoned, for he knew how handsome I had always told him he looked in a black coat. Oddly enough, he seemed about to pass me, and, involuntarily, I reached out my arm with an affectionate gesture to stop him. I was astounded when he passed right through it, and I could feel nothing. But as he looked over at me, I distinctly saw his lips move, forming the words, 'Dead or alive.'

"I even heard him say them, not with my outward ears but with some other sense, what sense I do not know. They were spoken as clearly as if they had been said with a normal voice. A moment later I felt my blood turn to ice. Hurrying over to where I knew Sherry was standing, I asked, 'Sherry, who passed you?'

" 'Let's go. I don't want to talk about it.'

" 'Sherry, you know whom I was coming to meet, and he had to pass you. You don't mean you didn't see him.'

" 'I heard him coming. I'd know that walk of his anywhere, and then he went right by only a short distance away. But, Karen, there was something wrong, something so strange about him that it scared

me to death. Then I saw him stand in front of you. What did he say?'
she asked.

" 'Come on. We can talk at home.' And talk we did, for half the
night, until finally we went to bed.

"The next day I phoned a relative of Jon's on some pretext. I had
not spoken with her in months, but almost immediately the conversation turned to Jon.

" 'You knew he had died, didn't you, Karen?'

" 'No! I've been out of town.'

" 'It happened last Friday while he was in South Carolina, and
we buried him Sunday in the family plot. He had become suddenly ill,
actually quite delirious toward the end. For the last hour before he
died, he kept saying over and over, "Dead or alive! Will I get there?" I
wish I could say he had a peaceful death. But poor Jon must have had
some terrible fear about reaching the hereafter that none of us ever
suspected. How I wish I had known it, so I could have led him to the
Lord.'

"Can you possibly imagine my own state of shock after that
conversation?"

---

*White Oaks, at 400 Hermitage Road in Charlotte, North Carolina, was built by
James Buchanan Duke and is also known as the Duke Mansion. Recently it has
been divided into condominiums and sold to private owners.*

EARLY HILL

Greensboro, Georgia

Houses are like people—they have a personality all their own. Some houses are sad; others, glad. Still others, however, seem to be inhabited by the spirits of those who once lived there, which is the way it has always been with the big antebellum house on Lick Skillet Road near Greensboro, Georgia. The white frame house with green shutters sits on a hill offering a panoramic view. Built in 1840 by Joel Early, brother of a governor, it was a fine house for frontier days in North Georgia.

When Joel brought his bride here, they named it Early Hill. Joel and Sarah's marriage was not blessed by children, and Joel himself died young. Years later, following Sarah's death after the Civil War, the house was sold to J. B. Y. Warner from Massachusetts. Mr. Warner did much to enhance the house's appearance, but the Warner family lived there for only a few years.

From then on, there was a sporadic succession of owners, but none ever seemed to stay. Townspeople knew when a family was living there, but they didn't know much about them or sometimes even who they were. People around Greensboro maintained that the reason no one would live there for very long was because the house was haunted. They talked of not just one ghost but several. In 1960 the house was purchased by Dutton and Carlene McCommons, natives of the area. Dutton, who had attended Presbyterian College at Clinton, South Carolina, was with the postal service, and Carlene, a graduate of Georgia College at Milledgeville, was a school librarian.

"We had heard there were ghosts there before we moved in, but we didn't believe in things like that," says Carlene. "All we could see were the possibilities for making the house just beautiful." When they bought it, the house had been empty for about twenty years. It had ten fireplaces but no wiring, no plumbing, and no heat. There was a wide center hall with two big rooms on either side and a front staircase ascending three floors.

31

Early Hill, Greensboro, Georgia. (Photo by Carey Williams Jr.)

The McCommons were both in their thirties at the time. Carlene was slim and small with dark brown hair and big green eyes; Dutton had black hair, a warm smile, and lots of energy. They did most of the work of remodeling and modernizing themselves. When they moved in, their daughter, Rosalyn, was eleven and their oldest son, Roger, was four.

"We had not been in the house long," says Carlene, "when we were told that people used to drive past on Lick Skillet Road and see someone rocking on the front porch. This was when no one lived here. But even more surprising was that, at this time in the house's history, there was no front porch. A lot of people told us about seeing this, and my husband would sometimes become irritated because he was a skeptic and didn't believe in ghosts.

"One night our son wanted to camp out and asked his cousin from town to come and spend the night. The front yard is about 400 feet from the road, and they decided to set up their tent out there with the opening toward the road. During the night, one of the dogs woke them up. Steve got up to see what was happening, thinking the dog might have treed a possum or coon, but the dog ran to him shaking with fear. He looked over toward the house and saw someone rocking on the front porch.

" 'Roger, do you all have company?' he called out to my son, waking him up.

" 'No, we don't have any company. Why?'

" 'Well, somebody is rocking on your front porch.' Roger came out of the tent to see. 'Look at him. He's dressed just like a frontiersman.'

" 'Oh, Steve, that's just our ghost,' said Roger, who then went back to sleep. But his cousin did not sleep nearly as well. Roger told me about it the next day.

"When the children were younger, our bedroom was upstairs, and one night there was a tornado watch on television," said Carlene. "We went to sleep, but about three o'clock in the morning, my husband waked up. Outside it was deathly still, and it was a stillness that was uncommon even out in the country, where it is always quiet. Dutton was afraid that it was the stillness before the storm and that a tornado was about to strike.

"He got up and looked out. You can see for miles from that hill. And he saw something floating around in the back yard. He came over to the bed and awakened me, saying, 'Carlene, I want you to look at something.' I went over to the window, and he said, 'Do you see anything in the back yard?' I nodded. He said, 'What is it?' I replied that it looked like a ghost to me, and he said, 'That is what I thought.'

"Later, we moved our bedroom downstairs, and one night, Roger kept hearing his sister crying. It went on and on, and he expected me to hear and come upstairs. Finally, he got so aggravated that he got up and went barging over to his sister's room to tell her to be quiet. To his astonishment, he found her bed empty; then it dawned on him that she was spending the night with a friend. He said he felt like a nut then. He didn't hear her anymore and finally went back to sleep.

"One day, when my youngest son was about four and the others were away, we were there by ourselves. Ross and I were in the kitchen, and I told him, 'Come on. We are going upstairs and straighten the bedrooms.' I started toward the stairs. He grabbed me and, hanging on for dear life, said, 'Don't go up there!' He was a calm child, and this wasn't like him. I said, 'Why don't you want to go upstairs?' He answered, 'There's a boy up there.'

"I thought he would forget about it if we did something different for a few minutes, which we did, and then I said, 'Now, we will go upstairs.' He said, 'No. There's a boy up there!' He did it several times, and I got disturbed because my husband had said that, if a convict from the nearby prison work camp escaped, he might come into the house. We were three miles from town, and there were no neighbors close by.

"By now, I had begun to wonder if someone had really escaped. When my husband came in the house about eleven-thirty, Ross was playing in the living room. I told Dutton about Ross's fears, and Dutton said, 'I'll go see if anyone is up there.' He started toward the steps, saying, 'I'll go up to the third floor and check out the storage rooms.' Ross came out and grabbed him and said, 'Don't go up there!' It bothered my husband that he was so adamant about it.

"The two of us looked at each other, and we really didn't know what to think. Dutton said, 'Take Ross in the kitchen and give him some milk and a cookie. Keep him interested for a little while.' I did, and he went upstairs to the third floor. In a little while he was back. 'Well, I've looked everywhere up there and didn't see anybody.' He went into the living room and told Ross, 'Ross, I have been upstairs to see the boy that you saw. I guess he went outside to play because he is not up there now.' Ross was apparently satisfied because he said no more.

"One day not long afterward, I was in the kitchen making jelly, and I had to stay and watch it. I wanted my daughter to come downstairs and do something for me. I went to the kitchen door, called Rosalyn, and ran back to the stove. I did it twice more because I could hear her humming and singing. I was beginning to get very aggravated with her. About twenty minutes later, when my husband came in, I said, 'Will you please tell your daughter to come down immediately? She is ignoring me.' He laughed and said, 'Why is that?' I told him that she was upstairs and wouldn't come down when I called her. Dutton replied, 'For the past hour she has been in the pasture helping me with the cows.' That incident gave me an odd feeling, for I was sure I had heard her.

"But one of the strangest things occurred one morning when I was alone. I had come back home after taking one child to kindergarten and putting another on the school bus. As I was making up the bed in one of the boys' rooms, I happened to glance in the large mirror over the dresser and saw the back of a little girl going up the hall. I thought some child must have come in the house. She had on a filmy pink dress. I went out in the hall to see where she was going, thinking it could only be Rosalyn's room at the end of the hall, but the little girl was nowhere to be seen.

"I recalled a story I had heard about the house that, while one of the families was living there, a young child had fallen from her swing and had been killed. Now I remembered the ends of a chain on a high limb. The links had been there so long, the wood had grown over them. Had that been the swing from which the little girl had fallen? Had the chain broken and dropped her to the ground to her death? How sad. And yet I shivered a little, too, for there was something eerie about hearing no footsteps and yet seeing that small figure going down my upstairs hall.

"While we were living there, and we lived in the house longer than any other family, a friend of mine who knew a medium suggested that we allow her to hold a séance. During the séance, the medium said there had been much sorrow in the house. We were in Rosalyn's room, and without knowing about the night Roger got up thinking his sister was in here crying, the medium said she could hear a child crying in this room. She told me about the child dying from the fall from the swing, and she pointed in the direction of that tree, the one with the chains on the limb.

"Later, I talked with some of the old people in the area, and they said, yes, the child had died after a fall from a swing. No one remembered the family name. In the twenty years after the Warners sold the house, it changed hands several times, and the death occurred during that interval. Actually no one lived in the house very long after the Earlys, and we wondered if one of the ghosts were from the period during which they lived there.

"Eventually the house grew too large for us, what with the children grown, and we built out here on Lake Oconee. There were some boards that were left after we had done some renovating at Early Hill, and from them my husband made two doors. One is to the attic, and the other leads to an under-the-stairs storage area. They are well hung and fastened, but on occasion they pop open, and no latch will hold them. A friend was here one day when the door to the storage closet squeaked as it opened. I remember her saying, 'I don't believe I could stand that.'

"We sold the house on the hill to a family named Murray, and they also heard and saw things while they were there. My daughter, Rosalyn, who has four children of her own now, came by the other day and said, 'Mother, the man who lives there now doesn't believe in ghosts, but he had better keep his eyes open in that house.' Everyone in our family saw or heard something."

———————

The house, on Lick Skillet Road in Greensboro, Georgia, will be available as a bed and breakfast inn by reservation only.

CEDARHURST MANSION

Huntsville, Alabama

There were champagne, caviar, paper-thin slices of Smithfield ham, canapés, smoked turkey, and more. There were ragtime, jazz, the strident notes of "Somebody Stole My Gal," and then the romantic ballad "Roses Are Blooming in Tripoli," which started many of the guests reminiscing. The musicians played on until shortly after midnight, and it was almost one o'clock before everyone had left.

Stephen Scott of Germantown, Pennsylvania, along with several others, had been invited to Cedarhurst Mansion in Huntsville, Alabama, for a house party over the weekend. Stephen was enormously pleased when he saw the house for the first time, for it was just the sort of home he had always envisioned southerners living in.

It isn't quite as sumptuous as the houses in *Gone with the Wind*, he thought as he dressed for the party, but it is a magnificent place. He was amazed at the architecture, for the rooms were immense, the ceilings high, and the walls fifteen inches thick. That was the reason his room was so pleasantly cool.

There was so much history here. In the early years, families lived close to each other, and that afternoon, he had visited the family cemeteries of the Ewings. Stephen S. Ewing had purchased the land here in 1823 from an Ebenezer Titus. What an odd name Ebenezer was. Were people ever named that anymore? It had some Biblical meaning, he thought. Well, he had seen many of the Ewings that afternoon. Not in the flesh, but at their graves. During the almost half a century that the family had lived in this house, those who had passed on to the next world were buried out there in the cemeteries.

He had rather enjoyed looking at the carved marble flowers and reading the inscriptions on the stones. Some of the epitaphs were admittedly flowery, but others had real feeling in them. A few words, or simply a name and date, sufficed now to characterize the deceased

Cedarhurst Mansion, Huntsville, Alabama. (Photo courtesy Cedarhurst Club.)

or the feelings of those left behind. Were feelings more genuine in the past, or were some of these epitaphs simply the custom of the period?

As he had arrived the night before, he was not tired. A disciplined man, he didn't know when he had last allowed himself to sleep as late as he had the next morning; it was nine-thirty when he made his appearance at the breakfast table. His host and hostess were already having their coffee, and soon the cook appeared, carrying covered silver serving dishes from which rose the steam of scrambled eggs, grits, country ham, fried chicken, and hot biscuits. With the exception of the white, tasteless grits, Stephen found everything absolutely delicious.

Of course, the life of a young stockbroker at a major Philadelphia firm was reasonably pleasant; and, even though his salary was a modest one, his parents had left him a comfortable income. He had never been seriously interested in any woman and was quite content to return alone, night after night, to the family home. The same lady that had helped his mother still came on each Monday and Thursday, as she had done for years, to straighten the house, change the sheets, and see that "Mr. Stephen" had an ample supply of clean attire. The first of October, Nellie put the down comforter on his bed; the last of March, she removed it and tucked in the lightweight summer blankets under the crocheted spread his mother had made.

Stephen liked people and fancied that he understood their feel-

ings. Someday, when he retired, he would write. The contribution he
would make to literature would be stories about people he had known,
stories filled with fresh, clever insights. Or he might even attempt a
novel of manners mixed with humor, something that savored of Ald-
ous Huxley. In any case it would be pleasantly predictable, a tale with
no violence and no disorderly, tragic lives with all their loose ends.
The unpredictable gave him indigestion, and he judged most people to
be like himself. They simply did not need another book that would
disturb them. Why couldn't more writers understand that?

He might start his writing career simply by doing an article now
and then, perhaps a story about Cedarhurst. This was a delightful
place, and such a story would give other Philadelphians an opportunity to experience vicariously a taste of what the Old South had really
been like. He was sure he could convey its gracious ambience in a
manner that would arouse his friends' envy.

His thoughts were interrupted by the sound of distant thunder.
The sheer white curtains at the open windows rippled as wind rushed
through the trees. A summer shower was on the way, and that would
cool things off nicely for tomorrow's activities with the other guests.
Stephen fell asleep contentedly.

When he awoke, it was to the sight of one brilliant flash of
lightning after another illuminating his room. Each sharp, explosive
sound was followed by a succession of gradually receding rumbles. He
had been responsible for supplies at an ordinance department during
World War II, and he recalled some explosives going off like that. The
lightning continued, and it sounded uncomfortably close.

In his childhood, when he would visit his great-aunt and there
was an electrical storm, the white-haired old lady and the little boy
would retreat to her big bed for safety. Piling feather pillows all around
them, she would hug him and reassure him that the pillows would
keep the lightning from striking. The curtains were now standing almost straight out, and gusts of rain had begun to pour through the
windows onto the beautiful, wide-plank floors. He thought of trying to
close the curtains, but at that moment there came a crash of thunder
so loud and so close that he felt it must surely have split the house
asunder.

Sitting bolt upright in the big four-poster bed, he felt like dashing out into the hall to get away from the lightning. Instead, he closed
his eyes and braced himself for the next detonation, but it did not
come. It was passing over, he thought, and he opened his eyes. Then
he closed them tight, and next he blinked, but it did no good at all.
For the girl was still standing in her long white dress over near the
windows.

He buried his face in his pillow, and, when he finally dared look
toward the windows, the girl was gone. With a deep sigh of relief,

Stephen pressed his arms close to his chest, hugged himself to keep from shaking, and started to lie down.

"Help me. Please, help me," came a young girl's voice, and there she stood, right beside his bed. Tall, with long, dark hair, she was very lovely, but Stephen was too shocked to appreciate her beauty.

"What do you want?"

"This terrible wind has blown my tombstone over."

"It has?"

"Yes."

"Well, I'm sorry." He was dimly aware that the wind had begun to blow again.

"You must go out to the cemetery with me and set it up again."

Now Stephen knew what had happened. He had been struck by lightning and was dead. He was just as dead as the girl who was standing there speaking to him. At that point he felt as if he were on a cloud drifting way up in the air and through the sky . . . he didn't know where and he didn't care.

The next morning was a glorious, sun-drenched day, and breakfast was served out on the side porch. It was nine o'clock, and everyone was there with the exception of one guest, Stephen Scott.

"Shall we wait, or shall we eat without the sleepy sluggard?" joked one of the men.

"Let him sleep on. He was too popular with the ladies, anyway," laughed another.

"I think I will go knock on Stephen's door," said their host.

At that moment the opening of the screen door to the porch was heard, and everyone turned to look. It was Stephen Scott, but his appearance was quite different from the night before. He was pale, and his hair and clothing were somewhat disheveled. Jokes about his late arrival evoked no answering smile.

"Did you rest well, Steve?" inquired his host.

"The storm woke me up."

"Quite a dilly, wasn't it?"

"Ghastly, I'd say." Leaving his breakfast almost untouched, he wiped his mouth with his napkin and rose from the table.

"Where are you off to, my friend?"

"I want to walk out to the cemetery."

"At this time of morning? We were out there most of the afternoon yesterday, but if you want to go, I'll walk out there with you."

When they reached the cemetery, Steve walked directly to the grave where a young girl was buried. He had read her name and age on the stone the day before. There, flat on the ground, lay the toppled tombstone of Miss Sally Carter, the sixteen-year-old sister of Mrs. Ewing. Miss Carter had died in 1837.

Both men were surprised, but, obviously, Mr. Scott was the more so. Pleading the sudden onset of illness, he terminated his visit to Cedarhurst well before nightfall. His host would always be puzzled by Scott's reaction to the toppled stone on "Miss Sally's" grave.

———————

In the early 1980s Cedarhurst, the historic Stephen Ewing house, and the land around it were sold. A developer has built private homes and town houses in the immediate vicinity. The restored house, at 2809 Whitesburg Drive in Huntsville, Alabama, now serves as a clubhouse for the Cedarhurst development. Its interior remains much the same. The cemetery was moved in 1983 to an undisclosed location. We wonder whether the move was even more unsettling to Sally Carter than a fallen tombstone. Will she appear some night to a guest at Cedarhurst and tell him she wants to return?

THE ELLEN GLASGOW HOME

Richmond, Virginia

It was an early spring day with the sort of balmy, delightful weather that might be expected in April in that former capital of the Confederacy, Richmond, Virginia.

The house that was being remodeled at One West Main Street had been built by a prominent tobacconist in 1841, two decades before the War Between the States. And although it was almost a half century later when Ellen Glasgow, the famous author, and her family moved into it in 1888, the Greek Revival house was still elegant. Four chimneys rose from the deck-on-hip roof, around the edge of which ran an elaborately molded cornice.

Now, long after the days of the Glasgow family and a succession of other inhabitants, the house had become the law offices of McCaul, Grigsby, Pearsall, Manning, and Davis. Constructed of lightly scored stucco over brick, the house had two full stories above its basement. On the day I was there, the front was covered by scaffolding, and two painters were at work within.

Most of us have a routine, and sometimes, when we depart from it, unusual or even frightening events happen to us. That was the way it was with our two painters, Jerry Bullock and Stan McIntyre, who were usually gone by four-thirty in the afternoon. But one day this was not the case, and that day, to them, would always be different from any other.

"Jerry, I'm going to stay until I finish this back room. I promised one of the lawyers that they could move their furniture back in here tomorrow morning."

"You want me to stay and help you, Stan?"

"No. It may take me half the night, but I'll get it finished."

"You sure now?"

"What do you mean, am I sure?"

"Nothing, just that . . . . Well, I guess you know what I'm trying to say, the noises and all."

Glasgow House was the home of a talented author but a haunted woman. (Photo courtesy the Valentine Museum.)

"Why don't you come right out and say it. You mean ghosts? Is that what you mean?"

"All right, all right. That's what I do mean. You make it sound like so much foolishness. I've been here more than once at night, so don't play games with me, old buddy."

"So have I."

"And you never saw them, you never even heard anything?"

"Oh, come off it. Maybe a noise once or twice, maybe a shadow or so over at the stair landing."

"A shadow? Lord a mercy! I wish it had been a shadow the night I saw it. I just wish it had. I almost knocked over my paint bucket, and you know you found the brush lying on top of it the next morning. Stop to clean it? I got out of here!"

"Just an excuse for leaving dirty brushes around."

"You're going to make me mad in a minute, Stan. You're the only man I'd stay in this house with after dark."

"I'll be fine."

"Okay, see you in the morning . . . maybe." Bullock slammed the back door behind him.

An hour later, Stan went out to his truck to get another can of paint. It was not there. But the job was going so well that he decided to call his son and have him bring a gallon of the color he wanted from his utility shed at home. Stan told his son where he thought it was in the shed and sat down to have a smoke until Ray arrived.

He sat on the floor, back against the wall, and thought. It was Wednesday. He and Jerry would be through and paid Friday afternoon, if Jerry could just keep himself together.

Ghosts, rot! Superstitious painters, rot! Why in the blue blazes couldn't he seem to find a helper who was normal? Maybe there weren't any normal painters. What was that verse about painters, preachers, and paperhangers? Well, it didn't matter. All that mattered at the moment was that he was getting sleepy, and Ray probably would not get to the old gray stucco house for at least twenty minutes.

He sat there, occasionally hearing small sounds, sounds that were probably like those in all old houses. Why should he feel uneasy? Then he became extremely frightened, for he was sure something had entered the room. He was more conscious of what it was *not* than of what it was. He was certain it was neither a person nor an animal.

It was a presence, and somehow he was convinced that the most evil force imaginable, some horrible, malevolent force, was in there with him. Scarcely breathing, not moving a muscle, he waited to see what would happen. Nothing did.

A little later he felt his head snap back. Caught up in a sort of trance, he had almost fallen asleep. Then he nodded off, and this time failed to catch himself. In what may have been sleep, he was certain he heard the tapping of typewriter keys. Then he was aware of the voice of a woman, and he began to listen.

"Who are you?" the voice asked. "You are here again; I know you are. Don't come any closer. Oh, go away!"

Then he heard a dreadful scream in the hall, and he leaped up and ran to investigate. It was the terror-stricken voice of a woman, and it sounded as if the gates of hell had opened and allowed her a shocking preview.

"Leave me alone!" the voice pleaded. "Who are you and what are you? Why do you come to frighten me? . . . Oh, good Lord!"

Stan thought he heard the body of someone falling at the second-floor landing and striking the first few stairs. He hurried into the hall, ready to race up the stairs and pick up the person who had fallen. To his relief, however, there was no one there. He stood perfectly still, looking up from the foot of the stairs, and his heart began to slow its wild beating. Then it began to pound violently again, for, as he stared up at the landing, he saw a most abhorrent sight.

Hanging a few feet below the ceiling in a diaphanous red glow was a face. There it hung, suspended in the air, a round, vacant face without a body attached. It was pallid, grotesque, malevolent. The bloated mask of evil stared down at him, and for a few horror-stricken seconds he stared back.

The next thing Stan was aware of were Ray's shouts and the boy's worried face close to his. "Dad, wake up! Wake up! Are you all right?"

Stan was lying at the foot of the stairs. "Where did it go?"

"Where did what go, Dad?"

"Didn't you see the face up there at the landing?"

"Dad, when I was out on the sidewalk in front of the house, I heard a woman's voice, and then I heard you start hollering, 'Get back! Get away from me!' The front door was unlocked, so I came in. I found you lying there at the bottom of the stairs. Who were you hollering at?"

"That's a good question, son. I suppose some would say ghosts."

"Ghosts of Miss Glasgow's little dogs, you mean? Like Jerry saw late one afternoon in the garden?"

"No, it wasn't the dogs. They'd never harm a soul."

"If it wasn't them, what was it?"

"Nothing. I don't want to talk about it, Ray."

And that was the last night either man ever stayed alone to paint. Stan and Jerry stopped work each afternoon at the same time, and together they would leave.

So many people have lived in the house that it is not hard to find others who have experienced ghostly manifestations at One West Main Street, which came to be known as The Glasgow House. Dr. W. Donald Rhinesmith, formerly head of the university center and later associated with the state library, was one of them.

"I am convinced," he says, "that there is a spirit in this house on occasion . . . . There is something walking around at night, walking methodically with a heavy tread, as if a troubled spirit is walking in her study. One night in her bedroom, I definitely felt a presence. It was about twelve o'clock, and I had just extinguished the light when I heard footsteps walking around my four-poster bed and over to the window. There I heard someone stamp their foot sharply on the floor. Why would she stamp her foot?"

If the foot stamper truly was Miss Glasgow, it could be one of many reasons: a hopeless love affair with a tragic conclusion; a broken engagement to a man she respected but, in the final analysis, refused to marry; an inability to accept her father's harsh, Old Testament God or, on the other hand, to establish any relationship of her own with the Deity; the frustration of her increasing deafness; and, finally, the unfairness of death's arrival before she had finished the novel she was writing.

Any one of these is a sufficient reason to stamp one's foot, particularly if one is a young woman who, according to her mother, was "born without a skin." The highly emotional and intense Ellen described herself as "devoured by this hunger to know, to discover some underlying reason for the mystery and pain of the world, for I had ceased to be a child . . . . I am alone now in this house where so many of us had once lived together." And about her lifelong quest for meaning, she said, "I was back again in the place where I had started, and in all my search, far and near, I had found nothing to which I could hold fast and say, here at last is reality . . . unless it was the little dog."

How did Ellen Glasgow feel about this house while, during the last years of her life, she lived here alone? She once said: "Ghosts were my only companions. This is not rhetoric. This is what I thought, or felt, or imagined while I stood there in that empty house with the few strident noises floating in from the street, and my eyes on the darkness beyond the thick leaves on the porch. I felt, literally, that I was attacked by fear, as by some unseen, malevolent power."

In her autobiography, Miss Glasgow tells about seeing a horrible vision on the stairs. "How old I was when I first saw that face without a body, I have never known. I may have been one or two years old, perhaps less, scarcely more. Fear may have choked back my words. But I do know that I, alone, saw the apparition and that I saw it hanging there . . . ." She describes it as a dreadful, disembodied face floating in the air, a vision that seemed to impress itself upon her for life.

What was the meaning of so frightful a sight? And how could a workman who had never known her appear to have shared this most terrifying and inexplicable phenomenon? Or did he encounter two ghosts that night—one of Miss Glasgow, the other of the "disembodied face" that had stalked this sensitive, talented woman from the cradle to the grave, perhaps even beyond the grave and into our time?

The large rooms once occupied by the Glasgows are now impressive offices. But the famous author's study still boasts the beautiful wallpaper, embellished with the red-tile-roofed houses of the Mediterranean, that she imported from England.

Those who have stayed in this house say that sometimes, while there late at night, they were sure they heard the clicking of keys on an old-fashioned typewriter in the upstairs study, where Ellen wrote *In This Our Life*, her Pulitzer Prize–winning novel. When they opened the door to the study, the tapping ceased, only to start afresh the moment the door was closed.

Does this old house play tricks on the imagination of those who stay here long enough? Or does a thwarted writer really return to work on a novel left unfinished when she died in her sleep that night of

November 21, 1945? It may be, for even now there is something clearly felt in that room. And why not the spirit of Ellen Glasgow?

———————————

The Ellen Glasgow home, at One West Main Street in Richmond, Virginia, is not open to the public. The exterior of the house may, however, be seen from the street.

BERKELEY HUNDRED

Charles City, Virginia

When I first saw him, the master of Berkeley was out picking up limbs that the wind's hands had stripped from ancient oaks. With his eighty-two years Malcolm Jamieson stood like one of the oaks, aged but sturdy. Beneath his shock of white hair, the blue wells of his eyes gazed out with humor and kindness.

No Virginian he, but from energetic Yankee stock, Malcolm Jamieson enjoys creating. Through both physical labor and imagination, clearing, and fencing, he wrests this gem of an early colonial plantation from the neglect of years following the Civil War. Malcolm Jamieson's imprint is everywhere. He has become an integral part of the place he has worked so much to re-create. In his head and on the drawing board are plans for next year and the year after. Visitors are looked upon not as intruders but as honored guests; Jamieson is certain they will share his enthusiasm for the place he loves, the timeless world of Berkeley.

In a very real sense Berkeley is the home of all Americans, for it is the birthplace of a signer of the Declaration of Independence and the ancestral home of two presidents. Over the past three and a half centuries this one plantation has seen more historic firsts than any other English-speaking settlement in America.

More than a year before the pilgrims arrived in New England, thirty-eight travel-weary settlers from Berkeley Castle in England landed in Virginia. After a perilous three-month journey at sea, the men of the Berkeley Company stepped ashore and, following orders from England, immediately fell to their knees to offer prayers of Thanksgiving for their safe arrival. The date was September, 1619. The occasion was the first official Thanksgiving in America.

By the spring of 1622, just as the Virginia settlement was gaining strength, the inhabitants of Berkeley met with sudden and violent

48

death during an Indian uprising. The Indians simultaneously invaded plantations all over the colony seeking to annihilate the English intruders. At Berkeley they succeeded; the original plantation never fully recovered from the massacre although it changed hands several times during the next seventy years.

The Harrison family acquired Berkeley in 1691; the history of this family and American politics blend together here like the sweeping green lawn and fields running down to the banks of the James River. The Harrisons were a family destined to contribute much to the growth of the young nation. Benjamin Harrison III established an extensive commercial center that included a shipyard on the James River. He named the spot Harrison's Landing.

In 1726 the fourth Benjamin Harrison built a three–story Georgian mansion which served as the base for his agricultural and trading activities. He married Ann Carter, daughter of the rich and powerful Robert King Carter, and their union began the web of kinship which was an integral part of the Virginia ruling class. Here in this house their son, Benjamin, was born and grew up to sign the Declaration of Independence.

A good–humored, gregarious man, Benjamin Harrison enjoyed the pleasures customary in England, such as fox hunts and fancy dress balls. His good friend George Washington was often entertained here. In fact, every one of America's first ten presidents enjoyed the plantation's hospitality. Two of these presidents came from the Harrison family—one was William Henry and the other, his grandson.

But by the nineteenth century financial reverses had caused the Harrison family to lose its hold on Berkeley, and Virginia was torn by the Civil War; General McClellan's federal troops occupied Berkeley after retreating from their siege of Richmond. On the grounds and fields surrounding this once proud manor house, the Union Army of the Potomac encamped 140,000–strong receiving supplies from U.S. Navy gunboats anchored in the Potomac River.

During that hot August a man named General Daniel Butterfield composed a haunting bugle melody called "Taps." It was a melody that soon drifted out into the darkness in one camp after another, into camps all over the world.

As Jamieson walked about picking up limbs on that warm autumn day, he thought about Berkeley's history and a panorama of scenes went through his mind leading from the past to the present, peopled by characters he felt he had come to know intimately. For some reason he found himself thinking of the young Harrison boy who had died during a severe electrical storm. When the rain and lightning began, Harrison had hurried upstairs to close the windows, his son following. Lightning entered an open window, striking the boy, who never regained consciousness. Strange—often as he sat in the living room telling the story, that one window, and none of the others, would come down with a resounding crash.

It was on that day that a white Oldsmobile station wagon rolled up to Berkeley and a family from Richmond, whom we shall call the Larrimores, began the plantation tour. Julie was more patient than her brother. Randy, not content to inspect all of the fine architectural details of the mansion and impatient to explore the farthest reaches of the plantation, slipped away during the movie about the plantation's history.

Randy always became restless when he had to tag along with his parents on tours of old houses, for he would rather be out tramping in the woods, slogging along in the muck beside a river or peering curiously into the musty dimness of an old barn. In the darkness of the room where the tourists were viewing the film on Berkeley, he had seized his chance to slip away. Perhaps, he could even melt back into the group as they came outside later. Meanwhile, he was off in search of adventure.

"This house was purchased by John Jamieson of Scotland who served as a drummer boy in McClellan's army fifty years ago," intoned the film's narrator. "In 1927 the plantation was inherited by his son, Malcolm, and together with his wife, Grace, they are responsible for the extensive restoration seen today.

"Window frames, floors and masonry as well as America's first pediment roof are all original. Much of the furniture came from Westover Plantation and the English silver, Waterford glass, and Chinese porcelain are authentic to the period. The famous Adams woodwork was installed in 1790. Berkeley's five terraces between the house and the James River were dug by hand using oxcarts and wheelbarrows before the Revolution."

Outdoors, Randy had already reached the third terrace and was contemplating which part of the plantation he wanted to explore first.

His parents continued to watch the film, unaware that he was no longer with them. "Today, the soybean and small grain crops that occupy five hundred of the more than a thousand acres of this working plantation are harvested with the latest in farm equipment. So, welcome home Americans, to a plantation where history lives today. We hope you enjoy your visit," said the narrator.

Julie and her parents filed out with the rest of the audience and she was just about to tell them Randy was gone when they saw friends. Everyone began talking and when Julie found their daughter her age was with them, she forgot all about Randy's defection. While they had been in the house there had been a summer storm and the sky had become quite dark, though it was not yet mid-day.

Randy decided in favor of the river bank. He, typically, had forgotten the time, and paid no attention to the darkening sky or even the first drops of rain. Over his head thunder crashed like freight cars colliding and flashes of lightning were all around him.

He was not easily frightened but he couldn't help but think of the story, how, long ago, Mr. Harrison and his son had been lowering one of the windows upstairs when the boy was struck by lightning and killed. Mr. Jamieson had said that often when he was relating the story of the boy being killed at the window, a noisy crash would be heard and everyone would hurry upstairs to discover that the open window had slammed closed.

Then, Randy saw a red-headed boy a few yards away beckoning to him. In a moment the pair stood together in a sheltered place where no rain was falling.

"This is a real cloud burst," said the boy.

"It's the lightning that bothers me," admitted Randy.

"I'll bet you're thinking about that story of Mr. Harrison's son being killed at the window."

"I guess I was."

"I used to think about it, too, when we were here and a bad storm would wake me up at night. A tent never seemed like much protection."

"You've camped out here beside the river?"

"Yes, many a night. My name is John. What is yours?

"I'm Randy. Say, you've got a nice drum there. Did it take you long to learn to play it?"

"No. You can't tune it but I like the rhythm. Reminds me of my father when he used to play the bagpipes. Of course, they carry a tune but there is a rhythm about their music and drums have it, too."

"I wish my father could play the bagpipes. Do you come out here to camp often?"

"The camping? Oh, that was a long time ago." By now the rain had stopped.

"I could come and camp sometime, maybe, if I asked my dad." And that reminded Randy he had better get back to the house quickly. He turned to say good-bye to his drummer friend but the red-headed boy was gone. He would get his father and together they would find him.

An excited Randy appeared just as they were almost ready to go into the little restaurant Berkeley maintains for visitors.

"Dad, I want you to come and meet my new friend!"

His parents were taking some pictures of the front of the house and Randy tugged at his father's arm to get his attention.

"Oh, all right," said his dad. "Where is this boy?"

"Near the river."

"Your mother would like to have lunch while we are here, but she can, probably, look in the gift shop for a few minutes. Let's go find him."

The pair took a path that led off toward the left while the boy chattered away.

"Dad, he was wearing a uniform and carrying a drum."

"Some of the people around here are dressed in costume, I suppose."

"He must be hot in that uniform."

"He is probably used to it." They searched until his father was getting impatient to go on to the restaurant, and were never able to find Randy's friend.

But when dusk falls across the emerald fields of Berkeley, because this is still a working plantation where barley, corn and other crops are grown; and the last tourist has left for his destination, Berkeley's real inhabitants return.

Although Randy did not know it, among McClellan's troops there was a lad born in Scotland, not old enough to fight a war but spunky enough to want to go. This brave twelve–year–old became a drummer boy, practicing until the alternate double strokes of the sticks upon his field drum produced a rhythmic, stirring call to battle. Its rumble could be heard through the trees like distant thunder.

Randy is not the only one to see him. Others have thought so, too. Some say he stands on the gently sloping hill several hundred yards above the James River near the Old Cemetery and by the split rail fence, a red-headed youth striking his drum softly and gazing out over the river. Others believe they saw the figure of a uniformed youth with a drum strolling beside the river bank and then back in the direction of the cemetery.

It may be that the young ghost drummer is the father of Malcolm Jamieson, present owner of Berkeley. For it was John Jamieson, born in Scotland, who came back years later and bought the plantation where he was once a drummer boy with McClellan's army.

Do rooms in old houses ever harbor sounds of past events, latent, ready to be touched off by some slight vibration, rare frequency or even an echo? Now and then, in the after–dusk, faint unison laughter, tinkling glasses and the murmur of voices has been heard. Could it be one of the many genial gatherings the rooms of this home have beheld?

There have been many reports of unusual sightings at this meeting place of historic events and people, such as a tall, gaunt figure, down at the water's edge walking slowly toward Berkeley. Lincoln himself had been to Berkeley twice during the war. Is he returning to

Berkeley Plantation is on Highway 5 at Charles City, Virginia.

review his army? On the way he is sometimes accompanied by a little drummer boy and together they turn right, up the path toward the hill with the split rail fence.

The two are obviously friends. Does the drummer boy remind President Lincoln of his own son? If you are among the very fortunate, you just might see two shadowy figures crest the hill some September evening, or hear the last faint roll of a drum as they disappear from view. And, while a late summer storm rumbles overhead, on the far side of the hill the Army of the Potomac will be passing in review for the President.

Berkeley Plantation is on Highway 5 at Charles City, Virginia. It is open year-round. To check hours you may wish to phone (804) 829-6018. (The restaurant on the grounds serves a delicious lunch replete with southern specialties.)

HOTEL IONE

Ione, California

At the foot of the Sierras in the California gold country nestles the small village of Ione, and on its main street is the most haunted-looking hotel you will probably ever see. The building is also quintessential Old West. You almost expect a gunfight to erupt at any moment, shots to ring out, and someone to pitch headlong right over that second-story balcony.

Millie and William Jones had longed to own this hotel for years; thus, when they were finally able to buy it, they could scarcely believe their good fortune. "We wanted to live here ourselves so that we could make it a hospitable place for other people to live, so we moved into the front three rooms on the second floor," said Millie. She is a delightful person, immediately warm and friendly. I enjoyed listening to her and, at the same time, absorbing the atmosphere of the hotel while we sat talking over a cup of coffee in the dining room.

When they bought the hotel in April of 1977, the Joneses were well aware that it needed extensive remodeling. So they began cleaning and painting, and they even moved the dining room from the rear to its present position at the front, where we now sat with a view of Main Street.

"It was a warm afternoon, June twenty-second, when I saw the first apparition," said Millie. "I was quite busy, for I was expecting the chamber of commerce for breakfast the next morning. Annie, our dishwasher, and I were the only ones there at that time of day. In the course of my preparations, I went back into the old dining room and was amazed at what I saw. Floating in the air in the center of the room was a cloud of what appeared to be smoke. The strange thing about it, however, was that it did not dissipate but seemed to retain what was a pyramidal shape except for a somewhat rounded top.

"At first I was afraid something must be on fire, but I checked and nothing had been left on the stove. For a little while I just stood

The Hotel Ione is said to be haunted by several apparitions. (Photo by Evelyn Prouty.)

there watching, almost hypnotized. Then I edged up closer and blew at it just as hard as I possibly could. I finally managed to blow it away. But in a minute or two, there it came, back again in exactly the same shape.

"As I watched it hover there, it began to vibrate. And as that smoky form moved back and forth, I began to tremble and could feel every hair on the back of my neck stand straight up. I don't know when I have been so frightened. I knew I needed some help, so I hurried and got the dishwasher.

"'Annie, there's smoke here in the dining room.'

"'There's nothing burning.'

"'I know, but what is that?' I asked, pointing at the pyramid.

"'There's been a lot of people in here smoking.'

"'Not today. Not a living soul has been in here. It's not like smoke after people leave a room. I just blew this away, and it came back in the same shape.'

"'Don't tell me that. I was just in here and fanned it with this towel, and it went away and came back the same way,' said Annie.

And then she said, 'I know what that is, but I don't want to say it, so we'll say it together.'

"'G-h-o-s-t,' we both said in shaky voices. Then do you know what we did? We ran.

"That was the first experience with our ghost, and, to the best of my knowledge, the spirit never came back in that form. During those first months that we were open, there was a customer who came to the hotel café regularly, a tall woman with piercing black eyes and straight, iron-gray hair that she wore in a large, soft bun at the back of her head. I remember her well.

"She had studied life after death and the supernatural and religious aspects of the afterlife. A very serious, scholarly lady she was, with all sorts of degrees. Sometimes we talked a little about ghosts when she was here and I wasn't busy, and I made no bones about what a fright the shape in the old dining room gave Annie and me that afternoon.

"'I will be glad to help you find out who it is,' she offered.

"'No, thanks,' I said.

"But she insisted on giving me her card just the same. 'In the event you have any problems, I will be glad to come and help you.'

"Of course, my reaction was, what could a puff of smoke do?

"As time went on, our dining room was completed. We had very nice flatwear and attractive placemats, and we put candles on each table. Let me tell you, there was a real thrill of accomplishment when we had it all ready for our first guests. There was just one problem, though, and it was so incredible that we didn't know what to do about it. Except for those at one table, the candles proceeded to light by themselves.

"We tried leaving the dining room and locking the door after us, but, when we came back in, the room was aglow with light. All the candles were burning. We managed to get most of them to stay out, but there was always one table where they would come back on, and that was the one right in the center of the room. This was the area where I had first seen the ghost.

"Of course, it was vitally important that none of our guests see this strange phenomenon. We were expecting the prestigious historical society from Stanford University. Since they had made reservations for a dinner party, we were going to make sure the candles did not relight. It was understood that if any guests left early, the candles would not be extinguished at their tables. Moreover, we decided that after everyone was gone, we would simply remove all candles from the dining room. That should solve the problem.

"But our troubles were not over. Shortly before our guests were to arrive, there was the most awful odor in the dining room, and I did

not know what in the world to do. Have you ever heard that spirits
sometimes have an odor that accompanies their presence?

"Well, I rushed over to the hardware store, got a lamp with an
aromatic candle in it, and proceeded to burn it in the dining room. In
a few minutes the odor was completely gone, and I was so thankful, for
everything smelled just wonderful. Everyone enjoyed a lovely dinner,
and they lingered on drinking coffee and talking. Midnight came, and
they still had not left. Finally, after the last guest had left, we took out
all the candles and locked the door. The next morning I came down
about five-thirty to fix breakfast, and the entire hotel smelled like
frankincense and petulie oil, sickeningly sweet.

"When I unlocked the door to the back room, the candles were
still burning. They had been moved from the top shelf of my grandmother's buffet to the bottom shelf, and they were burned completely
down to a tiny flame. That's when I called the lady who had offered to
come if I needed help.

"This hotel had burned down once, and by now I was quite
alarmed. We arranged for the woman who had studied the supernatural to come Saturday night at ten o'clock. I felt so silly even then that
I remember joking, 'It needs to be night, and I must have a black cat
under the table.'

"When the woman arrived, I brought the whole staff into the
dining room; then I thought it would be good if someone not connected with the hotel were present, too. I went out the front door, and
the first person I found was a gentleman from here in town who was
not intoxicated. I'm not saying that's unusual, but we were lucky because it was Saturday night.

"We all held hands and asked for a protective circle of faith from
God, and each person said a prayer to themselves for assistance in case
this 'thing' should come out. I had real reservations, and I said to the
woman, 'This could be frightening. It may be that I am exposing these
people to something dangerous.'

"'They are here of their own will,' she replied, and she began to
talk to the darkness all around us. Beside her on the table was a candle
she had blown out but which the apparition kept lighting. We had
divided up some paper into several pieces, and we each had a pen.

"'We know you are here, but who are you?' I heard her say.

"Nothing happened, and all of us just rolled our eyes around
trying to see each other's face in the dark. I really was afraid, I must
admit.

"'Come on! You are disturbing Millie Jones, and I want to know
who you are. You have a problem and we can help you.' There was no
answer.

"My heart began to thump so hard that that was all I could

think about. Then came a startling noise. The medium had struck her hand sharply on the tabletop. I started to cry out and said, 'I really don't want to do this.' But I heard the harsh, almost angry voice of the medium speak to me.

"'Hold on to your pen!'

"My arm hurt between my elbow and hand and got very, very hot as the pen wrote. I had to use my left hand to spread the pages out in order to hold the words. It was as if I were a child with a crayon, and a strong but invisible hand were guiding my own. The words formed on the paper said 'Mary Phelps.' I read it and heard my own voice saying, 'It fits myself,' and the medium said, 'All right, Mary Phelps, you have a problem. Now, how can we help you?' My hand began to move across the paper.

"Mary Phelps wrote that she lost a baby in a room fire in 1884. Other questions were asked, but no one got to write as I did. Someone asked what was the baby's name. The medium wrote 'Baby Jon.'

"You just held your pen, though you did not have to hold on tightly. It just wrote, and when Mary Phelps was through talking through you, your arm relaxed. I tried to trick her; I asked what was the room number. They have been changed often, and sometimes on New Year's Eve one of the guests, as a prank, will change a room number.

"I knew the hotel had not burned until almost ten years later, in 1893, and I was puzzled. My hand began going back and forth and back and forth, and I thought it was just relaxing from having been used as an instrument. Around the whole table nothing was happening, except that my arm would not stop moving back and forth, until the medium said, "You must be more specific, Mary Phelps. Which room?'

"At this question, the pen shot off the page in a sharp line, and then my arm went limp and dropped. I said, 'I just can't imagine what this could be.' Then I realized there were no room numbers then. In a moment my arm moved once more, and my hand, traveling across the page independent of my own will, wrote, 'Go where the wall is bent.'

"Two days later a member of our bartending staff said, 'Why, I know where the wall is bent. It's on the second floor right outside of Number 9.' We assumed that this must have been the room in which the baby boy, Jon, died and that it was not a hotel fire, it was a room fire. That's why it was 1884 rather than 1893.

"A year later, in October, I was cooking dinner, and eight people came in when we were almost ready to close. After they were served, the waitress came back to the kitchen and said, 'You have some fans in there who would like to meet the chef! I went in and curtsied, and they applauded. A young lady in the party was especially enthusiastic.

"'I just love this hotel. I don't know why we've never been here before, for we live in Calaveras County.'

"'That really isn't far from here. I hope you'll come again.'

"'Your waitress tells me you have ghosts?'

"'Yes, it seems to be a lady named Mary Phelps. When they heard that, the group went, 'Oooh!' And a Mexican gentleman among them turned to the young lady I had been talking with and said, 'I'm going into the bar and talk with your husband. I don't want to hear this.'

"The face of the girl turned very white. 'My maiden name was Mary Phelps. My grandmother and great-grandmother were named Mary Phelps, and at one time they lived in this old hotel!' You can be sure that I was as shocked as she.

"The next day she came back, bringing her grandmother, who held in her hand a small, black, leather-covered diary written in Gaelic. She translated as she read from one of the pages written by a Mary Phelps in 1884. The words were, 'I have recently lost my little son, Ian, in a hotel-room fire.' In Gaelic, Ian means Jon. The entire family came back and burned a candle in the dining room for the child.

"We heard no more from the spirit of Mary Phelps again except on October 26 of 1980, just after we did a television show for 'That's Incredible.' At that time Mary Phelps was seen by a couple from Sacramento who, I think, were hoping to see another apparition who had been mentioned on the television show and who appears here occasionally. There was once a workman living here named George Williams; he would work quite late, and he didn't always bother to lock his room. When he returned, he would sometimes find that an intoxicated friend was asleep in his bed.

"He would shake the bed until he could get the friend up, saying, 'I'm sorry. You can't sleep here.' George died, but we have had complaints from men who have occupied his room. They say that an angry old fellow has pulled the covers off them and tried to shake them out of the bed, saying loudly, 'I'm sorry. You can't sleep here!' I don't think he has ever bothered a woman in that room, only men.

"The couple from Sacramento did not see George, but the man's wife had a vivid experience. She awakened to see a woman dressed in black with a little bonnet on and her arms stretched out, pleading with her. 'Help me get my baby out of the fire! Help me! Please, help me!' said the woman. We assumed that it was Mary Phelps. The couple had retired quickly after arriving the night before, and we had no opportunity to mention anything to them about Mary. The entire incident was really most remarkable. But then, even finding out that she was a real person seems the strangest sort of coincidence, like something that would never happen in a million years," concluded Millie Jones, staring thoughtfully out at Main Street through the large plate-glass window of the hotel dining room.

———————————

The Hotel Ione, at 41 Main Street, P.O. Box 216, Ione, California 95640, is not far from Jackson, California. It has been remodeled recently, and, if you wish to stay overnight or enjoy a good meal, you will find it a convenient and picturesque stopover on your way to the California gold towns. Should you ask me whether I think it is haunted or not, all I can say is that I felt it was from the moment I stood in the lobby and looked up the stairs to the second floor. But others disagree, so perhaps you would like to see for yourself. For reservations, telephone (209) 274-4657. Best wishes for a good night's rest.

THE ALEXANDER-PHILLIPS HOUSE

Springfield, Massachusetts

It is doubtful whether the Society for the Preservation of New England Antiquities hosts many ghost-story programs. Even if it does, however, no other could be as unusual as this one regarding the Alexander-Phillips House, one of the most famous residences in Springfield, Massachusetts. The story was presented at a society meeting by the son of Mrs. Julia Bowles (Alexander) Phillips twenty-five years after her death.

Fortunately, one of those present at this meeting was Richard C. Garvey, editor of the Springfield *Daily News*. His interest in history and his writing skills combine here as he masterfully retells a ghost story both eerie and romantic. Garvey's source material was an account Mrs. Phillips wrote more than one hundred years ago, in 1886, and it was never made public until it was presented to the society. Garvey edited and paraphrased it for his own newspaper. With his permission, the story below is much as it appeared in the *Daily News*. (From an account written in 1886 by Julia Bowles Alexander.)

"When my father bought Linden Hall, I was very young, only seven years old, but my first recollection of the house is quite distinct. I was brought here by Father one afternoon when he came to talk over some business arrangement with the former owner, an elderly Southern lady who occupied it as a summer residence. She had been accompanied by her family of two sons and a beautiful daughter, a retinue of slaves, and a fine yellow coach drawn by thoroughbred horses.

"Soon we were established, and I and my young sister roamed at our own sweet will through the lofty rooms and the lovely gardens. The flower garden was the delight of my sister and myself. My sister was a strange child, fanciful and dreamy.

"Very soon I noticed the house seemed to have a special charm for her. Our dining room was then in the eastern wing and the library in the western. It is in this library wing that my story centers. We were still quite young when we learned that this library and the little bed-

This house was the scene of one of the most incredible courtships! (Photo by Bruce Roberts.)

room opening out from it had been lived in for years by a young man, one of the sons of the southern lady.

"During all this time, no one had looked upon his face. He was a very handsome fellow, they said, clever and fascinating in his manner, but like many attractive men with plenty of money, he had become dissipated and led a very fast life.

"Then, satiated with what he supposed to be the only pleasures of this world, he decided to isolate himself from his fellows and spend his remaining years in study and self-communion. My sister, Leila, was a peculiar, reticent child, and this story naturally made a great impression upon her. In the summer, when the old library was opened, she spent a great deal of time there, sitting at the window which looked out upon the garden and reading the queer old books, especially those related to the supernatural. The years of our childhood rolled slowly by.

"One warm Sunday afternoon early in June, when Leila was sixteen, she stood in the garden facing the library. She looked towards it, feeling drawn to do so by some strong impulse. There in the window sat a young man, and he seemed, to her, beautiful as a god. His large, dark eyes rested upon her with a gaze of burning intensity.

"She walked through the garden, around the pathway, and up the library porch steps, but on looking into the room, what was her amazement to see the chair in the window empty! She came immediately back to the rest of the family and asked what young man had been in the library. We laughed and replied that she must have been dreaming. She turned away from us with a troubled look in her eyes.

"Several days later, she came to me one evening and said, 'I have seen him again.' She told me she had stepped out upon the eastern porch for a moment and was astonished to see, standing in the driveway, a spirited black horse saddled and bridled with rich, silver mounted trappings. She turned her head and encountered again the face of the man she had seen at the library window. Before she had time to speak or even think, he leaned towards her, eagerly grasped her hand on which he pressed a burning kiss, and, mounting his horse in what seemed a flying leap, he galloped away in the dusk.

"As Leila related this to me, she was trembling with intense excitement. She begged me to say nothing of the matter to our parents, and I consented, though greatly troubled. About this time Leila became a somnambulist. One night I was awakened from a heavy sleep by a slight noise. I lighted my bedside candle, hurried into my wrapper and slippers, and reached the foot of the stairs just as a white figure opened the library door and glided out onto the porch. I was not of a timid disposition, but the ghostlike apparition was almost too much for my nerves.

"I recovered myself sufficiently to think that the figure looked like Leila. I hurried to her room. Both windows were open wide. The moonlight streamed in over the great fir tree, lighting up the whole chamber, and one hasty glance showed me that her bed was empty! I groped my way downstairs again and hurried out the library door. Midway on the garden walk, I met Leila. She was walking slowly with wide-open eyes and seemed utterly unconscious of my presence.

"It struck me as very curious that she was completely dressed in a soft white cashmere, her favorite dress, and her manner of walking was very peculiar. She seemed to be leaning toward someone. Her face was upturned with an expression of rapt attention, and now and then she smiled and moved her lips as if in speaking, but I could distinguish neither words nor sound.

"Without saying anything to Leila, I determined to speak to Mother, but I could not bring myself to speak to her about the two strange meetings of which Leila had told me. To my surprise, Mother appeared to think little of the sleepwalking and said she had been subject to the affliction when a young girl. I became so accustomed to her walks to the garden that I am sure I slept through some of them.

"The sultry days of August had come. It seemed to me I had never known such oppressive heat. For weeks we had no rain. At last, one evening we started to bed feeling a slight breeze stirring, and we said hopefully, 'Before morning, we shall have rain.' I must have slept heavily for several hours when I was awakened by a frightful flash of lightning followed immediately by a deafening crash. Before I could gather my senses, down came the longed-for rain in drenching torrents.

"My first thought was of the open windows throughout the house, and I flew from room to room closing them. On reaching Leila's room, a sudden flash illuminated the entire chamber and showed me that the room was empty.

"'Leila is out in the storm!' I cried out, and two or three of us took a lantern and went into the garden. Halfway down the walk we found her—her sweet life shattered by a thunder bolt! We bore her into the house and up to her bed. It was then that we realized she was wearing Mother's bridal dress, which we remembered having seen in an old cedar chest in the garret. She had arrayed herself in the quaint, old-fashioned gown and around her head had wrapped the bridal veil of antique lace.

"The cruel lightning had failed to mar her exquisite beauty. Not until all was over and we had laid her away in the grave was everything explained. A few days after the funeral I was in her room. On opening a little escritoire, I found a folded letter addressed to me in Leila's handwriting. The letter told me of the first time the handsome stranger in the garden spoke to her, and, when he did, it was a declaration of love! This is what he told her.

"'Leila, the power of love has drawn me from a far-off country to your side. Without question or fear, will you put your trust in me?" After quoting his words to her, she reveals her own plans, saying, 'I am going to that far-off country from which he came to me, and it may be many years before I shall see you all again.' It was her good-bye. This astonishing confession of Leila's was never known outside the family.

"Years went by and the city grew. Finally, through the constant raising of the street, the house seemed so low that Father thought it advisable to move it to the side lawn where it now stands. When the library wing had been removed, the workmen discovered in the low cellar beneath the bedroom the skeleton of a man. His bones were given decent burial near the graves of our own dead, and Father yielded to what he thought a strange fancy of mine and buried them next to Leila's grave."

The Alexander-Phillips House, one of Springfield's most famous residences, was built in 1816 according to the design of Asher Benjamin, then America's leading architect. It is closed to the public, but its exterior may be viewed at 289 State Street, between Elliot and Spring streets.

LILBURN

Ellicott City, Maryland

Highway 40 West, a few miles outside Baltimore, is bordered by the usual strip-development businesses, car dealers, restaurants, and taverns. But hang a left on Rogers Avenue, and you will find yourself abruptly entering another era, one where the clock's pendulum appears to have stopped sometime in the early 1900s.

Minutes later, the road will climb and then dip precipitously as you enter a narrow, populated valley between low, steep mountains. There, old-fashioned storefronts will stare at each other from either side of a narrow main street, which takes a sharp dog-leg turn at the bottom of the hill. You will have arrived in Ellicott City, a town teeming with people, many of them tourists. While some shop in the stores and others take pictures of mercantile establishments of the past, four oldtimers may just sit on the wide window ledge of an unoccupied bank building and exchange laconic judgments on the state of the world.

Ellicott City was once the terminus of the Baltimore and Ohio Railroad. In those busy affluent days, the four-story stone building on Main Street was filled with people. It was a hotel for travelers and a stopover for railroad magnates transacting their business far from home.

We were there searching for a house that had supposedly been the subject of interesting ghost stories. The newspaper clipping in my hand showed a portion of the house and gave the name of a family who lived there twenty years previously. No one whom we asked had heard of the family. Nor was the entire address given in the clipping; it mentioned only the name of the street.

We stopped to question a mailman, asking him if he could tell us the location of a house on College Avenue occupied by the Sherwood Baldersons. From our research we knew that the Baldersons were the owners in 1967, when a feature was written on the house in the

Lilburn, Ellicott City, Maryland.

Baltimore *Sun*. The mailman wanted to know why we wanted to know. Then he told us College Street was not in his area.

A middle-aged, dark-haired man who worked in the hardware store where we subsequently inquired had never heard of the family or of a haunted house on College Street, either. "Anyway, College Avenue is under construction and closed off except to local traffic. You can't go up there."

"I'm local traffic today," I replied on my way out.

We drove up the narrow road to the top of a hill. There we found a sign saying "College Avenue" and a barricade reducing the street to one lane of a hairpin curve. Fortunately, nothing was approaching, and we drove along safely. The newspaper picture we were relying on depicted only a small portion of an old, stone Gothic home. Worse still, the copy-machine reproduction I had run was dark and lacking detail. All the same, we had a feeling we would recognize the place.

A police car was parked just off the road, and we stopped to ask the officer.

"Sorry, I can't help you. I'm an out-of-town detective. It's boring as hell just sitting here waiting for someone to misbehave," he complained.

On we went. And then there it was, sitting back from the street on a curve, all three stories of it—dark and brooding in the late-afternoon light. Yes, it was the house in the picture. It gave us an eerie feeling, and there was something about it that made us feel we would have known it anywhere. We also recognized the tower where the windows were said to open mysteriously even after they had been bolted down. Despite a tiny, ferocious dog that I was afraid saw my ankles as the fresh bones he needed, nothing stopped us from making an appointment for a tour of the house and leaving unharmed.

We returned just as darkness was approaching, and I was impressed by both the three-story caretaker house and the three-story smokehouse, not to mention the large swimming pool and the house itself. The current owners, Mr. and Mrs. John Whitney, do not believe in ghosts. Still, they were kind enough to show us the various places in the twenty-room mansion where a ghost has reportedly been seen or heard.

Julie Whitney has done marvelous things with the house, which, during the 1930s and 1940s, was walled off into apartments. A woman of taste and discernment, Dr. Julie Whitney made restorations wherever possible and sought out wallpaper patterns from more than a century ago, when the house was built by Henry and Elizabeth Hazelhurst.

We stood in the center of the music room, admiring the immense mahogany piano placed there in the days of the Hazelhursts and, according to Julie, too heavy to be moved by later owners. Looking up at the mirror over the mantel, I saw that we stood in the midst of a pool of dark red, actually the reflection of an oriental carpet, surrounded by the dark, rich-looking furniture so much in vogue during the Victorian era.

Seven rooms had marble fireplaces, and the only thing unusual about the one in the music room was that a long piece of marble was resting across the top of the mantel. My first reaction was one of delight and admiration, for the flowers carved on it were exquisite. My next thought was that it once must have graced an elaborate tomb. Julie affirmed that it had, and I felt suddenly chilled, although the night was unseasonably warm. On the other hand, why not have these lovely things out where they can be enjoyed rather than in the solitude of a cemetery?

Julie hastened to say that most of the stories about Lilburn, which is the name of the house, are not true at all. According to her, many of them began during the time a family named Balderson lived there. During the four years the Whitney family had lived there, however, "I really don't know why we have such a difficult time getting people to deliver things to Lilburn. Can you imagine? Some people are actually afraid to come up to the house." She had actually seen none of the occurrences of which the Baldersons spoke.

By now we had reached the second floor, and she was showing us the immense bathroom and its dark, mirrored-tile floor full of reflections. In early years, this was a nursery. "I understand that some have heard the sound of children crying coming from this room late at night. And the owner before us says there were times when she was taking a bath that she would hear the door rattle and the sound of someone trying to break in," Julie said.

As we carefully mounted the steep, sharply curved stairway to the tower, we could hear Julie Whitney's voice floating back down to us. "Those stairs lead up here to the tower, and that is where many of the stories originated. People talk of footsteps being heard from the room below, also the sound of feet mounting those stairs we just came up, but none of us has ever heard them."

I looked back. It was apparent why no footsteps could be heard. Not only this room but the stairs as well had been covered recently with luxuriously thick, rose-hued carpeting. One wonders whether it is best to hear the footsteps first, or just be surprised by the specter.

"Here in the tower room is where the windows have been said to come open mysteriously, and, actually, they still do, despite these metal latches. But we are sure it is a weather phenomenon and connected with the change of seasons," continued Julie.

Walking over to the casement windows, I stood beside her and looked at the fasteners, which were steel. Each latch slipped down into a notch, and I jiggled one of them to determine whether it would move readily. I could not move it and was uncertain as to how the expanding and shrinking of either wood or metal could cause closed and latched windows such as these to be found at times standing wide open. But surely there are rational explanations for things like this, and weather can do strange things.

Built of gray stone, Lilburn is an imposing four-floor Gothic Revival style house with high, peaked gables, tall chimneys, and graceful arches. It is on the State Register of Historic Houses, and last year it was part of the historical society tour of homes. "Of course," Julie said, "I went to every effort to have the house perfect, and I conducted the ladies through myself. I was astounded when one of them came up to me and said that the flowers in the vases kept rising up and down and what was I doing to cause such a thing. Another said that no one would ever get her to come to this house again. So, you see how absolutely ridiculous people can be."

"Did you notice this stairway? It is rather peculiar, because it should have gone through here where this landing is. Instead, it simply ended. They say that a young man hanged himself from the balustrade here above the downstairs hall. What a dreadful thing! But like the smoke in the library, I am just quoting what I have been told."

"The smoke in the library?"

"This is the room. I believe the original owner smoked cigars, and people say that sometimes the odor of cigar smoke is very noticeable in here." As I entered the room, my hostess went back out into the hall, and I stood looking around. There was no aroma of a cigar, nothing out of the ordinary at all unless . . . was that a small mound of silvery ashes beside the easy chair? I bent over and pinched it with my thumb and forefinger, and it left a smooth, gray deposit on my fingers.

"So, as I'm sure you can see, all of this is really more talk than anything else," said Julie Whitney. She walked us to the door, where we thanked her for the tour of her home and said good night. Even with a tiny, dark streak on my white cords where I had rubbed my fingers, who was I to say that this grand, old, gray-stone house has ghosts in its tower? Or cigar smokers in its library? Or perhaps even the wraith of some restless lady, returning to reclaim the carved marble decor that once held down the top of her tomb?

The lights flickered off in the house as our little white Honda wound around the curved drive. The moon illuminated the gray stone of the tower and was reflected in the windows. But despite the warmth and hospitality of our hostess, I thought about that little old lady who finished her tour with the historical society but was not eager to return to Lilburn again!

––––––––––––

Lilburn, of Ellicott City, Maryland, is a private home and not open to the public.

MORDECAI HOUSE
AND
THE ANDREW JOHNSON HOME
Raleigh, North Carolina

S urely a city that has no ghosts could be a dull place. And was Raleigh, North Carolina, such a city? It seemed, for a while, that it might be. No one at the Cameron Village Branch of the Raleigh Library knew of any ghosts in the capital city. There were no clippings of recent newspaper stories in the files that reported a local apparition. Oh, from the standpoint of ghostly presences, everything was all right in Fayetteville, Asheville, Wilmington, and even Charlotte. But not in Raleigh. Raleigh had politics but no ghosts . . . unless you count the bed in the Governor's Mansion from which a mysterious rapping sound was once rumored to emanate. As this occurred while a Democrat was in office, however, Republicans were not inclined to regard it too seriously.

Nor are ghostly presences sufficient in themselves. Being one of the few states not included in a United States Tourist Bureau list of those with haunted houses, North Carolina was understandably miffed. On one side was South Carolina, with Alice of the Hermitage; to the west was Tennessee and the Bell Witch; and most humiliating of all, on its northern border was Virginia, with an entire register of haunted houses!

Such a situation could make a proud state, full of colorful history and mountain scenery, appear almost prosaic. Sure, it had a beautiful ghost hitchhiker, the famed Brown Mountain Lights, and Joe Baldwin's ghost at Maco. There was, however, surprisingly little else that was noteworthy . . . but wait, new specters have come to the rescue.

Not far from the heart of Raleigh is a small historic park called Mordecai Square, and its most impressive building is the large Mordecai Manor itself with its many wings. Also on the square are a quaint building once used as a law office; a village chapel; a tiny house in which our seventeenth president, Andrew Johnson, was born; and a small, early building used for an office by the Raleigh Historic Properties.

On the afternoon I called Historic Properties, good fortune was heaped up and spilling over. Ms. Terry Myers was there. Did she know of any ghost stories in connection with any of the historic properties? Indeed, she did! But not so fast. What sort of person was Ms. Myers? It was reassuring to learn that she was a knowledgeable, charming lady full of enthusiasm about North Carolina history. A former schoolteacher from Arizona who inspired her students to do special history and folk-lore projects, she moved to Raleigh and had been working for Historic Properties for several years. The first ghost-story account is of her own experience.

"One November afternoon I wanted to complete a project, and, without realizing it, I worked on well after everyone else had left. When I realized it was time to leave, it was dark outside, but I've never been afraid here." This was the beginning of not one, but two, unusual stories.

The day I talked with her was also in November, and golden leaves covered the trees in the square. The buildings were awash with that intense color from the late afternoon light, and, if there was ever a perfect time to visit Mordecai Square, this was the day. The lanterns on the tall posts along the street cast their warm, yellow light on the buildings, and the restoration seemed to come alive. One could imagine women in these houses engaged in meal preparation, and the lawyers had doubtless retired from the front of their law offices to sip a glass of sherry before supper.

Just as autumn is a time between summer and winter to pause and reflect, so, too, seems this period at dusk a time of recollecting, of ruminating by the hearthside upon the events of the day.

On the afternoon of her story, inside the Historic Properties office, Terry Myers was putting the papers she had been working on to rest. Arising from her desk somewhat stiffly, for she had been sitting there longer than she realized, she slipped into her dark blue coat and was ready to leave. On the porch outside she could smell the wood-smoke from someone's fireplace, and then her trim navy pumps were crushing fallen leaves noisy as tissue wrappings. The sound was a lonely one. No, not really lonely, she thought, just natural, nature shedding its garment from the previous season.

Now Terry was approaching the lamppost in front of the tiny, gambrel-roofed house in which President Andrew Johnson was born in 1808. This early nineteenth-century environment had become so real to her that sometimes modern street lights could be almost jarring. She had left late like this before, but tonight at the edges of her mind she was aware that somehow, something was different. What could it be?

Had a light been left on that should have been turned off in one of the buildings, or was there a glow through the crack of a door that should not have been left ajar? Were the parking lights of a car along the street reflecting in a window?

In any event she knew that she felt uneasy. Was someone else here on the square tonight, and was that person carrying a flashlight or a lantern? This thought caused her to stop, for, if that were the case, she would stand back beside the office building in the darkness until the person passed. Whoever it was would likely walk along from the direction of Mordecai House, past the stone marker in front of the Andrew Johnson Birthplace, and head toward the street.

She heard the furtive rustle of leaves and shrank back against the building. The sound grew closer, and she could feel the thump of her heart. Then there was a sudden flurry in the leaves just a few feet from her, and she almost ran. Instead, she stayed perfectly still. More rustling. Perhaps whoever it was had seen her and knew that, in a moment, she would be flushed like a frightened bird from its hiding place.

Suddenly, something white darted from the blackness past her. She almost fainted until she saw with relief that it was only a large, white cat, probably chasing its prey. She stepped back on the path, and it was then, for the first time, that she looked squarely at the single downstairs window in the tiny house that was the birthplace of the seventeenth president. In that window was the source of her uneasiness.

Suspended there, as if held in the center of the small window by an invisible human hand, was a candle, its bright flame silhouetted against the blackness of the room within. It seemed to hang there interminably, and she stood staring at it. There was no reason for anyone to be inside that house with a candle. Then, with the flame appearing ready to go out at any moment, the candle began to move away from the window, and within seconds it was gone—but not for long. A moment later it reappeared, this time in the second-story window.

Terry was genuinely frightened. Someone or something was in that house. She turned and ran toward the safety of the street. When she had reached it, she stood there for a moment and looked back. She was just in time to see the candle, until then burning steadily in the tiny upstairs window, go out as suddenly as if it had been extinguished with an old-fashioned candle snuffer. Was it a ghost? If so, Terry had seen enough.

"That is the only time I have ever had anything happen to me that was eerie or out of the ordinary. I was later told that realtors had seen the same thing. By the way," continued Terry, "Rosa Burt has an unusual story, if she will tell it. Rosa is the housekeeper at the Morde-cai House."

Mordecai House dominates the square. It was built in 1785 by a

Birthplace of President Andrew Johnson at Mordecai Square. Lighted candles have been seen at the windows. (Photo by Nancy Lee Roberts.)

planter named Joel Lane, but it acquired its name and fame from one of the first Jews to settle in Raleigh. A gentleman of education and means, Moses Mordecai married the Lane's daughter, Ellen. Mordecai and his bride retained William Nichols, a noted Southern architect, to remodel the house. Behind a Greek-Revival double portico is a double-doored entrance hall and five large rooms. It was the earliest example of this type of architecture to be built in Raleigh.

Most historic homes are furnished with pieces donated or purchased that are compatible with the period of the house, but the furnishings here were actually the belongings of its early families. They owned and lived with these portraits, pictures, books, and furniture. Perhaps their attachment for some of these things may be the key to Rosa Burt's unusual experience.

Rosa is not a superstitious person, but she will never understand an experience she had one morning at Mordecai House. There is a long hallway down the center of the house, and at the end of it is the library. On the right of the hall is the parlor; on the left, the dining room. Rosa remembers exactly what happened.

"I was there one afternoon, cleaning when the house was closed to visitors, and I was just finishing up in the dining room. There I stood in the doorway, wiping down the woodwork, when I saw what I supposed to be one of the docents [guides] walking up the hall toward me from the library. The lady wore a long, black, pleated skirt and a white middy-type blouse with a black tie.

"I stood and watched, for I thought she might be one of the docents, and I was puzzled because they don't usually come on days when I am cleaning. She didn't even look over at me as she came down the hall. I remember thinking to myself that she might at least nod her head or act like I existed, but she didn't. She came walking along just like she owned the place, head in the air and looking straight ahead. Then, when she was right opposite me, she turned and went through the parlor doorway across the hall.

"While I was out in the hall working, I think I was expecting her to make some noise or come out any time. But all was quiet and she did not reappear. Finally I decided to see what was going on. I walked over to the parlor door and looked in. When I did, there wasn't a soul in there. That room was empty as it could be. This gave me a real start, for I knew I had seen her go in, and, if she had come out, she had to pass by me. There wasn't any other way.

"You can't imagine how this stayed on my mind, and I kept thinking about it. I knew all of the women who were guides, and she certainly was not one of them. But even though she wasn't one of the guides, I knew her face was familiar. Finally I thought, why, she looks just like Margaret Lane. She was a pretty thing, and I've seen her

Who was the phantom lady seen recently in the historic Mordecai House at Raleigh, North Carolina, and will she reappear? (Photo by Nancy Lee Roberts.)

picture many a time when I was cleaning." Margaret Lane was an early resident of the house.

"Sometimes, even now, when I'm working, I find myself going over and over it in my mind, thinking, how did it happen?" Rosa looked down the hall in the direction of the library. "All I know is that she went into that room and never came out of it. Mmmmm. If I saw that sort of thing often, my nerves wouldn't take it!"

To this day, Rosa shakes her head and wonders.

Mordecai House and the Andrew Johnson Home are at 1 Mimosa Street, Raleigh, North Carolina 27604. They are open to the public. Admission is free, but hours may vary. More information may be obtained by telephoning (919) 834-4844.

PIRATE'S HOUSE
Savannah, Georgia

The Moores strolled along the Savannah waterfront most of the afternoon, intrigued by the variety of shops housed in the brick buildings that had once been cotton warehouses. About five-thirty they began deciding where to have dinner.

"Let's ask one of the natives," suggested Marion. Her husband groaned.

"Do you remember that little hole in the wall in San Diego? The last time you asked a native, it was terrible."

"You have to take some risk if you expect to find adventure."

"I don't want adventure, just a decent meal."

"Look at that man over there, alone in the faded blue dungarees. I'll bet he would know."

"All right. You ask him, and then I can blame you later."

The seaman was sitting on a bench, sifting through a number of fishing lures. "Visitors, are you, and you want to know where to get a good meal? Well, I suppose that depends on your taste and your wallet. Where are you folks from?"

"We're New Englanders, from Massachusetts. Both of our families have always lived on the coast," said Marion.

"And mine, too," said the seaman.

"What do you think of the Pirate's House restaurant?" asked Jack Moore. "Maybe I ought to take my wife there. She's always saying that one of her ancestors was a pirate."

"Well, join the club," the seaman replied. "My grandfather used to say that we were descendants of Captain Bartholemew Roberts, one of the most audacious buccaneers of his day. They called him the Crimson Pirate because he liked to wear colorful clothes."

"We really ought to introduce ourselves. I'm Marion and this is my husband, Jack Moore."

"Glad to meet you. My name is Matt Roberts. You were asking about the Pirate's House restaurant. The food is fine. I eat there myself

77

The Pirate's House at Savannah was once a home for seafaring men such as Flint and Blackbeard. It is now a well-known Savannah restaurant. (Photo by Bruce Roberts.)

now and then, but sometimes some of the goings on bother me a little." He looked down at the lure he was tying on his line.

"You mean loud music, that sort of thing?"

"No. I didn't mean that."

"Well, then, what bothers you?"

"It's other things. Things like . . . well, it's hard to say."

"Like what?" interrupted Marion Moore.

Roberts just looked down at the knot his weathered hands were tying and shook his head. "Don't pay any attention to an old sea dog like myself. You folks will like it. The place has an interesting atmosphere."

"Is your boat tied up near here?"

"That's her right there. The *Nora Jane.* She is named after my wife, although I'm a widower now. I take her out every morning about sunup, and we're back here by late afternoon. Some days the catch is quite good. It certainly beats teaching at a university."

"Where did you teach?" asked Jack.

"Michigan State."

"And you just left it all?"

"I was down here on vacation one summer and decided to stay. My family has been in the commercial fishing business here for years."

"Have you ever regretted it?"

"No. I have too many seagoing ancestors to want to spend my life in a classroom."

"Well, look here. How about being our guest for dinner?"

"You folks don't need me along."

"It would be a real treat for us. You can tell us about Savannah, and you and Marion can swap pirate stories."

"You've talked me into it. Let me go by my place and change."

"That's great. Marion and I will have a few oysters at a raw bar and then meet you in front of the Pirate's House at seven o'clock."

At seven they were waiting in the parking lot, and up drove Matt Roberts in his Wagoneer. The Pirate's House is a rambling, old frame building on East Broad Street, not far from the waterfront. The house was once an inn for Savannah seamen. Its shutters are painted blue, a custom along the coast of South Carolina and Georgia, for the color blue is believed to be a protection against evil spirits.

"Well, Marion, you and Matt are entering the old haunts of your ancestors," joked Jack Moore as the trio walked up the wooden steps of the porch.

"This part of the city was like the Barbary Coast in California," said Matt after they had ordered. "It was an area where men were drugged and shanghaied; and when they awoke, they found themselves on a vessel out at sea. Not far from this house the Savannah River forms a half moon, and yet it's still fairly deep. Ships that drew twelve feet of water could ride within ten yards of the bank. My grandfather said that pirates who came here were on the lookout for men and boys to kidnap. They would take them out through an underground passage to the river and load them, unconscious, into a small boat to take them to the ships lying in wait only a few yards offshore.

"As time goes, it has not been so long since Savannah swarmed with sailors night and day. They were men of all nationalities, and many were pirates who swaggered along the streets of the city sporting cutlasses and swords or a brace of pistols. The LaFitte brothers made Savannah their headquarters for awhile, and Jean LaFitte married a local girl named Mary Morton."

"I want to know more about that underground passage," said Marion.

"It's here, just as it's always been. But let's eat our meal while it's hot."

They were almost through when Marion said, "Jack, what is all that loud, rough talk I hear?"

"What in the world are you talking about?"

"It sounds as if some coarse, crude sort of man is shouting."

"Do you mean that party at the table over there? They are just having a good time. Don't let it upset you."

"I'm not talking about them." Marion glared at him. "Jack, don't you hear that man's horrible, loud voice calling out?"

"I do not." Matt place his hand soothingly on Marion Moore's arm. "I'm not sure I hear what you do, but I do hear an undertone of voices at times."

"Of course, anyone can hear that."

"Marion, tell me what words you hear, not just an undertone of men talking but the actual words."

"I'm not sure I can do that, but let's all be quiet for a few minutes, and I'll try." For a little while they ate silently, and then Marion's face clouded. "I hear it again."

"What are you hearing?"

Her face turned white, and she shook her head. "Matt, do you know where the opening to the underground tunnel is?"

"Yes."

"Jack, do you mind waiting here for the check? I want to see where that passage is."

"Go ahead."

Marion followed Matt Roberts out of their dining room into another and still another until they came to a small storage area.

"It's back here," he said, pushing some furniture to one side. And there, in front of them, was a hole in the floor. It was the mouth of a tunnel. Marion stood staring at it.

"I don't think we should try to go down there. Do you still hear anything?" asked Matt. She shook her head, and he turned to go back.

Suddenly, her hand seized his arm. "Now! That's the voice. Do you hear it?"

Matt stepped over to the edge of the tunnel, and his face changed. "Who in the Devil . . . that is one of the most evil voices I've ever heard, bar none!"

"Matt, he is calling me!"

"He is not calling you. Tell me what you hear."

"He's calling M'Graw over and over. That was my maiden name. I must go down there!"

"No, you are not. He doesn't mean you! See if you can make out anything else."

"'Darby . . . Darby M'Graw' is what he is saying." By this time they were joined by Jack Moore, who stood listening.

"What else do you hear?" persisted Matt.

"This is crazy! Let's get her out of here," interrupted Jack, seeing his wife's terrified face.

"Wait a minute, Jack. Now, listen hard and tell me what else you hear, Marion."

She stepped closer to the tunnel. "Just the jumble of voices. No. He's shouting again!"

"And he's saying?" prompted Matt.

"'Fetch aft the rum, M'Graw. Fetch me the rum!' That's what he's saying, but why my name?"

"He isn't calling you. Let's get her outside, Jack."

"What in Hades was all that about, Matt?"

"Yes, what was it about," echoed Marion weakly.

"Marion, tell me something," said Matt.

"What is it?"

"Do you have unusually sensitive hearing? Do noises bother you that don't bother most people?"

"Yes."

"I can't explain what happened back there, but perhaps we can put some of it together." Matt spoke quietly, his voice subdued. "There are many stories about the Pirate's House, but probably the best authenticated one is that the infamous Captain Flint died there and that his ghost still haunts the rooms of the old building. It is not surprising his ghost cannot rest, for Robert Louis Stevenson wrote that, in sheer wickedness, 'Blackbeard was a child to Flint!' On the night he died, it is said that he was delirious, and he shouted raucously time and again to his former shipmate, 'Fetch me some rum!' The name of his shipmate was Darby McGraw."

"But it seemed to come from the passageway," said Marion, puzzled.

"You heard it when we were sitting at the table, too, didn't you?"

"That's true, I did."

"Have you had experiences like this before, hearing sounds other people cannot hear?" asked Matt.

"Yes. There have been times that were similar."

"My father was like that, and I share it, but to a much lesser degree. Haven't you seen a flock of blackbirds covering an entire tree-top, the tops of several trees, all singing? Suddenly, at exactly the same moment, there's a fluttering of wings and they all soar into the air at once. Above the racket, there must have been some signal, and they all heard it."

"Yes, yes, I've seen that."

"I'm a seaman, and I know a school of whales playing on the surface of the water with the curve of the earth between them will sometimes dive simultaneously. The signal has sounded, but it is too deep for us on deck to hear, although we may feel the vibrations."

"And that is what you think about the voice in the Pirate's House?"

"I only know there are sounds most human beings cannot hear. They are too deep or too high."

"But I know I heard that voice."

"You have an unusual gift, Mrs. Moore," said Matt, looking at her with something approaching awe.

The Pirate's House, now a famous restaurant, is located at 20 East Broad at Bay Street in Savannah, Georgia, and is surrounded by a ten-acre historic area. The Herb House, said to be the oldest building in Georgia, is part of the complex. For reservations, telephone (912) 233-5757.

LOUDOUN

Philadelphia, Pennsylvania

I t was on the early 1940s, just after Miss Maria Dickinson Logan died, and yet I remember it as clearly as though only a few months had passed. My wife and I occupied a room on the house while I was looking after the place. I don't think either of us will ever forget the nights we spent there, when I was a temporary caretaker.

"If you are familiar with Loudoun, you know it is the house with four white columns across the front, and that it stands at the top of Neglee's Hill, where Germantown Avenue passes Apsley Street. Miss Logan willed the house to the city of Philadelphia to be maintained as a museum.

"One night, about the middle of December, my wife was awakened by a feeling of intense cold and felt a strong breeze blowing full upon her face. She sat up in bed and saw to her great amazement, standing at the foot of the bed, a tall column of cloudy white light extending from the foot of the bed straight up to the ceiling. Staring at it spellbound, she noticed that the light fell across the bed so that she could see the pattern on the spread, and it also illuminated the dressing table and mirror. She was extremely frightened, pulled the covers up over her head, and lay there petrified. Finally she gathered her courage enough to look out, and, when she did, the room was in darkness.

"When I woke up, she described the light as having been similar to a tall column of a filmy material with a strong light emanating from it. I could hardly believe this, and she was worried that I might believe it was either a dream or something that had occurred in a half-wakeful state. But she seemed so certain that I told her to awaken me immediately if she saw the luminous column again.

"My wife and I both shared the feeling that there was a presence in the house. Whether it was that of Miss Maria Logan or her brother, who lived here with her for many years, or even some earlier owner, we had no way of knowing. My wife thought it was Miss Logan, and

Loudoun House, built on a hill over the bodies of Revolutionary soldiers, has its own strange story. (Photo courtesy Germantown Historical Association.)

sometimes, when she would find a book or magazine out of place, she would say, 'I wonder if this is something Miss Logan was reading.' When she would say that, I always had an eerie feeling.

"A few weeks later I woke up early in the morning to find my wife calling to me.

"'Hurry! I want you to see it.'

"'See what?' I was still half asleep.

"'That thing is here again.'

"I rose up in bed and looked in every direction, but the room was extremely dark, and I saw no sign of any light. We then turned on the light, and my wife said that, while I was asleep and just before she woke me up, there had been a bright, globular light at the foot of the bed. At first it was the size of a ball, and then it began to increase in size until it must have been three feet in diameter and was higher than the height of the bed. Again, there was the filmy appearance, and the inside glowed as if there was a light in it.

"She had tried to awaken me but could not elicit anything but a groan, as I seemed to be in a deep slumber. All the while, the light was directly at my feet and partly over the edge of the bed. Afraid that it might grow into something dangerous, she shook me vigorously. The light kept on shining and growing larger, but, when I did wake up and answer her, she said it collapsed at once and sank down into strange folds similar to those of an accordion. This time I took her story much more seriously, and, after I turned out the light, we watched together until daybreak. It did not reappear.

"I was coming back to Loudoun one day when a neighborhood boy stopped me for a few minutes to talk. It seems he would be delivering his newspapers early in the morning, and, on several occasions in the winter while it was still dark, he had seen lights flashing on the darkened front windows of the house. I think he really wanted to know whether I had seen anything, and I didn't let on that I had.

"A month or so must have passed, and we had begun to think that whatever had happened was an isolated event and would occur no more. Then, in the late summer, I woke up to my wife's hand gently pressing my shoulder and her whisper, 'It's here.' 'What is it?' I called out. I rose to a sitting position, and there, at the end of the bed before me, was an awesome cloud of glowing light about four feet in diameter, suspended in air. It was only a few feet away from me. As I watched, it began to float upward like a gas balloon, and I thought that it would hit the ceiling. It seemed to go straight up, and when it reached the ceiling, rather than stopping, it went right through it. I know I cried out, but it was an exclamation of wonder rather than of fear.

"I checked the room to see if light was coming in from any source, and there was none. Passing the door, I tried the night latch and found it on. Then I said to my wife, 'Tell me from the beginning what you saw.'

"'I first woke up when I felt the bed vibrate due to a shock, which may have been under it, or it may have come from someone striking the surface of the bed,' she said. 'There at the foot sat an elderly woman in a white dress looking very calm. Her clenched fist rested on the footboard, and I had the feeling she had just struck the bed. She sat there bathed in light, a light so bright that it illuminated the room. I tried to wake you, and when you called out, the figure began to dissolve into the luminous cloud. First the head went, then the body, and a moment later the cloud drifted up to the ceiling and disappeared.' The last part of her story was exactly as I had seen it myself.

"On the next occasion, the figure of the woman stood by my side as I slept. My wife roused me, and, as I woke up, it vanished with a flash of light as bright as the flare of a match. After my wife and I left Loudoun, we came back a few years later and stopped to talk with the caretaker. He had seen lights on several occasions but never anything as distinct or as close to him as my wife and I had experienced."

Children tell of seeing someone sitting on the sun porch, most often a little old lady. Mrs. John W. Farr, who was head of the Friends of Loudoun, relates, "Some of the neighbors say that Miss Logan is guarding the property. And, I must say, a number of things have happened for which there are no explanations."

On one occasion Mrs. Farr's committee members arranged some heirloom plates in a china closet. Returning several days later to continue their work, they found there were no plates. Eventually, the plates turned up on such a high shelf that it took a ladder to reach them. Both the china closet in which the plates had been arranged and the house itself had been securely locked. When she was ready to leave one day, Mrs. Farr discovered the large pocketbook that she had left in the drawing room was missing, and a search through the house proved fruitless. Two days later, there was the bag, in plain view in another room. Nothing was missing from it.

Dick Nicolai, Fairmount Park Promotion Director, has heard a story over the years that might account for the missing bag. A playful ghost called "Willie," a member of the Armat family who died quite young, is said to return and move small objects about.

The live-in caretaker has never had a problem with break-ins, and neither did the caretaker before him who lived on the premises for twenty-seven years. That is unusual. But it is possible that fewer people try to break into houses with a reputation for being haunted.

Then again, could there be more than one spirit residing on Neglee's Hill? At the time of the Battle of Germantown, wounded American soldiers were carried to the top of the hill on which Loudoun now stands. They were later removed in wagons to Philadelphia. But many soldiers carried to the hilltop were dead or dying, and they were ultimately buried there. Is it possible that, when the cold winter winds make dried leaves rustle, the restless spirits of some of those young men, dead before their time, may rise and walk again?

Loudoun was built by Thomas Armat in 1801. He called it Loudoun after the name of the county in Virginia from which he had come. The house is reminiscent of those of Virginia, and he must have had many pleasant memories of his early years on the South. Armat, a distinguished philanthropist and a man of strong faith and inventive mind, was one of the founders of St. Luke's Episcopal Church. He was the first to suggest coal for heating and the first to patent a hay scale. The house museum, containing much of the home's original furniture, is open to visitors on Sunday afternoons. It is located at the northwest corner of Germantown Road and Apsley Street in the historic Germantown section of Philadelphia, Pennsylvania. Further information may be obtained by telephoning the museum at (215) 842-2877 or the Fairmount Parks Commission at (215) 686-2176.

REED HOUSE

Asheville, North Carolina

I was longing for adventure that rainy December afternoon in Asheville, North Carolina, and how much closer it was than I had realized! The place I was searching for, Reed House, was in the Biltmore area. Turn off Hendersonville Road onto Erwin Street, I had been told. This is exactly what I did as I headed straight up a wet, black ribbon of a road right into the sky. At least that is the way it seemed on my way to the top of the low mountain. To my right, in the distance off to the south, were purple-blue mountain ranges. If the sun were going down, I knew they would be washed with crimson, but not on an afternoon like this. Today was gray and rainy, and the mountains ringing the city of Asheville were shrouded in mist.

I was looking for a certain bed-and-breakfast place that, I had been told, had a ghost story connected with it. As I drove along looking at the homes, there on my right appeared an immense old Victorian mansion, looming up out of the fog. The sign read, "Reed House." Perched on a steep hill, Reed House overlooks Biltmore House, the famous estate owned by George Vanderbilt and the setting for several films, including *Being There*. Reed House was built nearby in 1892 by Samuel Harrison Reed, one of Vanderbilt's lawyers. The huge, pale yellow edifice boasts an elaborate turret between its two wings, a wrap–around piazza, ten fireplaces—one in each of its five guest rooms—and sixty-two windows. It is on the National Register of Historic Places.

One look at Reed House and the thought at least crosses your mind that it is haunted. It has all those fine characteristics that a haunted house should have. Am I jesting? Only partially. But when you see a dainty, white-haired lady in bright blue cords and a blue sweater flashing a warm smile at you as she holds open the door of the glassed-in side porch, you forget about ghosts. On that dismal December day I visited, she looked like a small, bright patch of sky. Marge

The Reed House, Asheville's haunted bed-and-breakfast, has a ghost whose favorite pastime is playing pool.

Turcot extended her hand in welcome. Obviously she enjoyed sharing her home, and I had an immediate impression that I wouldn't be a stranger there long.

"The first night we slept here," said Marge, "we were awakened in the middle of the night by the sound of heavy footsteps on the back stairs. I have a teenage daughter, and it occurred to me that she might be trying to sneak someone into her room, so I waited about ten minutes and then went upstairs. She was sound asleep, her brothers were asleep, and there was no sign of anything anywhere. For several years, anytime someone slept here who had never been here before, we would hear the sound of those same steps on the back stairs. We got so that we would know we were going to hear it anytime we had visitors or new people in the house. Since the steps have been carpeted we don't hear them, and if they are still there, they must certainly be only a soft thud in the night, which no longer wakes us up.

"In those first weeks I recall talking with my mother in Minnesota and saying, 'Mother, so many things are happening in this house that I think it is haunted.' I am so practical and down-to-earth that mother was really worried, but all she said was, 'Marge, don't you think you may be working too hard?' "

The most unusual experience has been reserved for Marge herself and has seldom happened when others have been in the house.

On the nights she has been alone here over the years, she has sometimes heard the sounds of a ghostly pool game being played in the
small room behind the parlor.

"It begins with my hearing the break when the balls go. Then
the balls hit each other, and, in a moment or so, there would be the
crack of one ball striking another. I thought it was one of the kids
when they were living here at home. Then I would hear a key open
the front door, and a voice would call, 'Mama, I'm home.' I would say,
'Well, who is here already?' The answer would come back, 'Nobody,
I'm the first one,' and yet I knew someone had been here playing pool.

"Look at that pool table. The balls are all in perfect order. When
we have guests, I seldom hear the pool game going on, but even then,
sometimes one ball will disappear. Just last July a ball was gone for
about two or three weeks, and then, suddenly, it was back again. My
husband came in from work and said, 'Where in the world did you find
that ball?' I went in and looked, for I hadn't found it either, but there it
was in the rack, right in the number one spot where it belonged."

Mrs. Turcot's children have grown up and have been living in
other parts of the country for a number of years now. "When the
children were at home and slept across the hall from each other in the
Circus Room and in the Lavender Room, strange things happened.
One would be in bed and see the door across the hall open and close.
They would get up to speak to their brother or sister, glad they were
still awake, too, but no one would even be in the other room. This was
a frequent happening. I'm a nurse, and, when I first moved in, I just
thought, well, I don't believe in any of that stuff.

"But I'm sure you would like to tour the house, and we can talk
more about our ghosts later. Reed House is so large, it was once four
separate apartments, but we have restored it to the original ten rooms.
This is the parlor, and that enormous piano has rosewood legs. Over
there is the fainting couch for Victorian ladies who were laced rather
too tightly. This is the pool room, and it is from this room, between
the parlor and Lawyer Reed's library, that we have heard many of the
ghostly noises."

As we reached the landing of the front stairs, my hand touched
the smooth, rounded top of the newel post. It gleamed with a satin
patina, the result of almost a century of hands like my own passing
over it as their owners went up and down these stairs.

This was one of the most ingenious and modern houses of its
day. Even when Reed House was built, in 1892, there was running
water from a windmill in the back, and there was a gravity system.
There are two sets of stairs, the front stairs for family and guests and
the back for the use of the servants. It is on these back stairs that
footsteps are most often heard. Upstairs there are four bedrooms currently available for guests. A spacious front room has white-iron twin

beds with white lace spreads, lace curtains to match, and a soft, pale blue wallpaper.

One of the daintiest rooms has white wallpaper strewn with lilac flowers, and its five tall windows look out over the treetops. There are two comfortable rockers, a wicker cradle with a doll, and even a chamber pot. But my favorite is the small room at the back, by far the coziest with its delightful, deep blue, flowered paper; rose-colored carpet; old trunk; dark, glowing woodwork; and a fire already laid and awaiting the touch of a match.

My tour complete, I was ready to curl up in front of the cheerful fireplace in the family room downstairs and listen to Mrs. Turcot recount the events that have convinced her that some who once lived here at Reed House have never left.

"You know how it is when you have a scientific education, you think everything has a cause. It may have a cause, but that doesn't mean I understand it. On our first Christmas here, in 1973, we had the tree in the front parlor and were telling stories around it, about noises and all the things that happen in this house. Many of our guests who worked at the hospital like ourselves made fun of us, but, in the midst of their laughter and scoffing, the Christmas tree fell to the floor.

"No one had slammed the door, jumped, or even sneezed. Nothing. The tree just toppled over on top of several guests. The next day I asked my son to wire it so it would stay up. He put it back up without wiring it at all and said, 'Mother, look at this.' He jumped on the floor several times. 'This tree doesn't need wiring; it's solid as a rock.' The tree stayed up for a solid month, for we never got around to taking it down until sometime after New Year's.

"One evening my husband and I were convinced we had uncovered the identity of our pool player. We were sitting out on the porch when we heard the sounds of a lively game going on in the house. We were sure it was our youngest son and his friends practicing up to play with the older boys. About that time, and to our amazement, he came walking up the driveway with a basketball under his arm. The three of us hurried in and went from room to room, checking the entire house, only to find all the doors locked from the inside, including the one that led out onto the porch, which we had secured when we came in from where we had just been sitting.

"None of us have ever felt threatened. This ghost is not a scary type, but on the other hand, it is certainly something we cannot understand or explain."

Who could the pool-loving specter be? Might it be Samuel Reed himself? Pool or billiards was the game of wealthy men a century ago, and they would commonly retire to enjoy a game after dinner. There were two pool tables at the Biltmore House, which was built at the same time as the Reed House. Reed undoubtedly had joined in games at his employer's home on occasion and had friends who played pool with him here in his home.

He had nine children, but only four lived to maturity, the rest dying in infancy. Could these games be a family reunion for a spot of pool? Reed and the children are buried not far away in Asheville's Riverside Cemetery, where Thomas Wolfe is also buried. There is no way to be sure until that time comes, if ever, when the ghost pool player decides to make himself known. One feels almost apologetic because this ghost is a lightweight. He is neither tragic nor threatening and can best be described as something of a "good-time Charlie."

The house possesses some of the most interesting and characteristic features of the Victorian era. The beautiful tiles around several of the fireplaces are from Italy, and each bedroom has its own unusual mantel and style. There is even a secret passageway, another turn-of-the-century Victorian feature, which adds a strong touch of mystery.

"We have guests from Italy, Switzerland, New Zealand, England, Germany, and all over the United States and Canada," says Mrs. Turcot. "In the late afternoon we serve wine and, each morning, a continental breakfast." Since Mrs. Turcot is health-minded, it is not surprising that one of her breakfast specialties is low-sodium biscuits or muffins, and she has received many compliments on them. She leafed proudly through the guest book in the front hall, and I noticed the number of names and the variety of places from where her guests came.

"When we close during the winter months, at first I really miss not having people here. The house seems so empty. Now and then, we hear one of our ghosts; but, you know, ghosts are no real company at all." There is no denying that.

Mrs. Turcot is president of the Preservation Society of Asheville and Buncombe County, and she and her husband both have full-time jobs at St. Joseph's Hospital. This makes it hard to spend unlimited hours restoring the house, but before-and-after pictures indicate many hours dedicated to this labor. Reed House is listed in the National Register of Historic Places and has always been considered a local landmark by the Asheville Historic Resources Committee.

Reed House, at 119 Dodge Street, Asheville, North Carolina, is open May 1 through November 1. Like many bed-and-breakfast places, the house is in the process of being restored to its original beauty. The rooms currently are 40 dollars, double occupancy, with no extra charge for ghosts. For more information, telephone (704) 274-1604.

SHIRLEY PLANTATION

Charles City, Virginia

It was a cold autumn night, and Coleman Webb did not waste time window-shopping along the windy New York City street. The NBC newscaster was eager to reach the warmth of a restaurant, where he could relax.

He glanced at the travel bureaus that he passed and wished he were in the Caribbean. As his gaze fell upon the display in the window of the Virginia Tourist Office, he noticed an oil painting. Depicting a beautiful and arresting young woman, the painting was on loan from Shirley Plantation, a famous James River house. He paused, drawn by the face in the portrait. In that brief moment he was to see something that would puzzle him for a lifetime.

As he stared at the proud, lovely face, he began to think that the picture was moving. Of course, he was either more tired than he realized, or it was an illusion. Despite the cold, however, he stood there as if transfixed. Was it really swaying, or was he imagining it? He continued to watch.

Webb was now beginning to shiver from the cold. Much as he hated to leave, he could not stand there all night in front of that travel office and freeze to death. A few minutes later, seated at the little French restaurant, he ordered his favorite dish. While he ate, though, all he could think about was the painting. What might cause such a thing? Was some mechanism inside the travel office responsible? Or was it possible that he had been mistaken?

His plan when he left his office had been to take a cab from the restaurant to the theater, but now he decided that there was only one way to determine whether his eyes had deceived him or not. He would walk back the same way he had come and look into the window again. That should satisfy his curiosity once and for all.

A few minutes later he stood staring into the same window, and this time the movement was much more apparent. He decided he would try through concentration to stop the motion, and he tried this

The lady of Shirley—is she at rest now that her portrait has been restored to her plantation home? (Photo by Bruce Roberts.)

with all the strength he could summon. The portrait continued to sway to and fro. Webb reported this unusual phenomenon of the swinging portrait on his news show, and it created quite a stir. The painting was of Martha Hill, a Virginia belle born at Shirley Plantation on the James River.

Some months later the tourist office was being redecorated, and the portrait hung in a closet with the door locked. A young woman from Long Island had the key. There was so much noise coming from the closet that people in the office had trouble working. The key was retrieved, and the portrait taken out. Some damage had occurred to the frame, and it was sent off to Richmond to be repaired. It was during that interval that investigators from Duke University arrived, eager to see it. Unfortunately, they had come at the wrong time.

Martha Hill's portrait now hangs in a prominent position over a handsome mahogany chest of drawers in one of the downstairs bedrooms at Shirley Plantation, and it looks down on tour groups that go through the mansion. Insofar as anyone is willing to admit, her spirit is at peace with the world, and the astonishing antics of the portrait have ceased. Undoubtedly the facts that the Hills had been at Shirley since 1649 and that it was Martha's birthplace must have contributed to her restlessness while she was in New York. Many Southerners living there long to return to their home state but are unable to find a way. Martha must have felt that she had only to kick up her heels a bit to get back to Virginia, and she was right. Now she is home.

Ten generations of the same family have lived at this great plantation since 1638, when Edward Hill received the tacit surrender of pirate Richard Ingle. With the marriage of Elizabeth Hill to John Carter, the plantation's ownership was passed on to the Carter lineage, and young Hill Carter became the sixth master of Shirley.

His advanced methods of farming made Shirley prosper, and no outsider would have noticed buildings in need of repair. During the Civil War, after the Battle of Malvern Hill, the wounded men of General McClellan's army "lay all about this lawn, and all up and down the riverbank," according to Louise Carter's memoirs.

When the Union nurses ran out of bandages, Mrs. Carter pulled sheets from cupboards and even off beds and tore them into strips. Soup was prepared in Shirley's kitchen, and hundreds of loaves of bread were baked for the wounded. Men who did not die there in the shadow of the willow oak were finally moved to Union hospitals by Union ships, which took them aboard at Hill Carter's wharves. General McClellan sent Carter a letter of appreciation.

Meanwhile, Mary and Hill Carter's sons, Charles and Hill, Jr., were serving in the Confederate Army. The following April, Louise wrote in her journal: "We heard the rumble of a heavy vehicle on the walk in front of the house, and it was all Mama and I could do to go out on the portico and ask who was there?" Young Hill Carter had just been killed in action at the Battle of Chancellorsville, and his brother, Charles, was bringing Hill's body home to Shirley. "General Lee wrote Papa a touching letter about Hill's death. He said, when he wanted the truest, most faithful soldier to send on special duty, he used to order that Hill Carter and John Pelham should be sent to him."

Even as the war was being fought and Shirley lay in no-man's land between opposing troops, the plantation was being visited by tourists. A note remains among the home's papers that "Mr. Carter will be visited by a son of President Lincoln, who goes to your plantation to look over the grounds—get some flowers for his mother. Mrs. L. is at present sick on board my boat, the *River Queen*, Wm. Bradford, Commanding." It was dated March 28, 1865.

When the war ended, Hill Carter was seventy years old. He had endured problems enough to have wiped out a man of less determination. Even with slaves deserting daily and a shortage of farm labor and having to fight off scavenging Union soldiers, his fields were still productive, and his account books show he had not fallen into debt, as had so many of his less fortunate neighbors.

Another major war, the third in three centuries, had washed across Virginia, and once more Shirley Plantation had survived.

———————————

Shirley Plantation, on Highway 5 at Charles City, Virginia, is open to the public daily. It is fitting that the current owner is a direct descendant of the original family and bears the name Hill Carter. The portrait of the restless lady is now at peace. It hangs above the mantel in one of the rooms and may be seen on the tour. For more information, telephone (804) 829-5121.

WINCHESTER MANSION

San Jose, California

A luxurious black carriage cruised slowly through one of Boston's old neighborhoods, through what had once been a fashionable street lined with grand houses. Paint peeled from most of them now, and soot from coal-burning furnaces gave the neighborhood a bedraggled look. The driver leaned over and peered at the front of each house, trying to make out the numbers. One of the more depressing houses was painted mustard color with cream trim, and it was here that the carriage paused.

A few seconds later the driver stood on the porch, turning an etched, brass doorbell. Not even the most curious eyes peering through the windows of the neighboring houses could tell whether anyone was waiting in the French carriage. Gray curtains at the windows of the gleaming black vehicle were mysteriously drawn to prevent anyone from looking in.

There was a jarring, metallic sound as the driver twisted the bell several times. Then he stood there, not knowing whether anyone would answer. What a miserable neighborhood, he thought. How strange and inappropriate this trip was just a day after the great man's funeral. Whatever could Madam expect to find here?

At that moment the knob turned, and the door was pulled suddenly open. The driver stepped back, startled. There stood a tall woman with deep-set, olive-colored eyes in a pasty white face shaped like a hatchet. Her black hair was pulled back severely and wound in an immense twist on top of her head. She was wearing a long, somewhat shabby brown dress and a black shawl. The driver's usually impassive face must have reflected shock, for the woman looked at him harshly and then stared out at the fashionable carriage in front of the house.

"She will have to come in herself, you know. Tell her that Mrs. Raven will see her."

He went back to the brougham, opened the back door, and

It could be a nightmare to find one's way out of the Winchester House, particularly for the terrified young girl in this story. (Photo courtesy Winchester House.)

relayed the message just as it had been given him. A gloved hand emerged, and he offered his arm to help a tiny, heavily veiled woman attired in black step down from the carriage. She was followed by a younger lady, who wore a hat with a soft veil wound about the brim. The driver, Charles Farnham, accompanied them to the front door, and here the older woman made a peremptory motion for him to return to the carriage. He did so as the pair disappeared into the house.

Farnham was uneasy. It was not just that the expensive brougham was attracting attention in an unsavory neighborhood; it was the appearance of that woman. There was something about her that was evil. More than an hour passed, and yet his two passengers remained inside. He was tempted to go up and ring the bell to be certain that they were all right, but he didn't really dare . . . not yet, at any rate. He restlessly pulled out a smoke. Rain was beginning to fall in a fine, light drizzle. What were they doing inside that house all this time? he asked himself.

It was getting dark now, and he hadn't seen any lights go on inside. He had almost gathered up his courage to check and see if Madam and her niece were all right when the front door opened. "Miss Margaret" came out first. Sarah Winchester, her aunt, turned back toward the darkness of the doorway to speak to someone he assumed was Mrs. Raven. Why didn't the woman light some lamps? Miss Margaret, as everyone called her, was like Mrs. Winchester's shadow, doing her bidding without question. Since the death of William Wirt Winchester, son of Oliver Winchester, the "rifle king," she had been her aunt's constant companion.

This was the first of many trips Farnham was to make during the winter months of 1884 from the Winchester mansion at Hartford, Connecticut, to the shabby street in Boston. Sometimes Margaret would accompany her aunt. On other occasions Sarah Pardee Winchester would go alone. She never seemed herself after a trip to the Witches' Palace, as Farnham had begun to call the house in his own mind. After the last visit, Mrs. Winchester appeared extremely frightened, clutching Margaret's arm and talking hysterically.

"Do you know what she says, Margaret? She says the money William left has a curse on it!"

"Why would she say that?"

"She says the spirits of all those men and women that were killed by the Winchester are haunting the fortune and that they are going to harm me."

"But there were lots of people killed by the rifle. Soldiers, Indians . . ."

"Mrs. Raven says the worst haunters will be Indians, and that there is only one way to keep them from getting me!"

"What is that?"

"She says it can be done only by my getting a larger house that will attract good spirits, and they will keep away the evil ones. It must be fixed up according to their wishes."

"But who is going to know their wishes, Auntie?"

"She will guide me about that."

Farnham, who was doing his best to hear the conversation, shook his head. People said her husband had left her $20 million. It was hard for him even to imagine how much money that was. But despite the money, he had begun to feel sorry for her. Poor woman, the death of her husband must have affected her mind.

On their last trip to the house in Boston, just as they were about to get into the brougham, something huge and white flew past them, and Mrs. Winchester screamed. Farnham thought it must have been a large owl startled by their carriage lights. He and Margaret tried to soothe her, but Sarah Winchester almost collapsed, and it took their combined efforts to get her into the carriage.

The next day, to everyone's surprise, Mrs. Winchester announced that she was moving to California. Farnham overheard her tell Miss Margaret that she believed the owl had been a warning that they must leave Hartford, and, from now on, "the spirits themselves will lead me." Of the staff given the opportunity to move, none accepted but Farnham, who was unmarried at the time.

At San Jose, Sarah Winchester bought an eighteen-room house. Her first move was to hire twenty-two carpenters to commence immediately building a wing on the house. Landscape gardeners arrived and began to plant a towering hedge that shut off any view of the house from the road. Seven Japanese gardeners fertilized and pruned the hedge so that no one could possibly see through it.

Before they had left Hartford, Mrs. Winchester used to talk with Farnham occasionally. Now she never spoke, and all instructions for him, the servants, or the workmen had to come through Miss Margaret, her niece and secretary. After a year or so, Farnham found that he could scarcely remember Mrs. Winchester's features, for the veil put on for mourning was never removed except in the presence of the Chinese butler who served her dinner. Once, years later, Farnham asked Won Lee what Mrs. Winchester looked like now.

"She little old lady . . . look like shriveled plum," replied the butler, shrugging.

From the first days of her arrival in the new house, carpenters and masons were at work seven days a week. There seemed to be no hurry about completing many of the projects, and the workmen wondered why they were asked to be there on Sundays, holidays, and even Christmas Day. They had no idea that a Boston spiritualist had promised Mrs. Winchester that, as long as hammers rang out day and night, nothing bad would ever happen to her. The good spirits would keep the bad spirits away.

Sarah Winchester was holding her séances alone now in the séance room, sitting with her pen and pad to write down the spirits' instructions for her life. The message she believed she had received was that there were two tasks she must accomplish. The first was a fearful one. She must somehow keep out low and depraved spirits who would try their utmost to harm her. Her second task was to please the good spirits with whom she would one day take her place when she moved on to the next world. Both of these goals were expensive. The good spirits could be pleased only by the most expensive furnishings, and therefore she saw to it that the decor of the rooms was worthy of a royal palace.

It was vital that none of the evil spirits should ever get into the small, bare-walled séance room, which no living person but her entered until after her death. Her way of getting there was through a labyrinth of passages and rooms. To elude and frustrate the evil spirits

who sought to follow her, she spent hours planning unusual and unex-
pected construction tricks for the carpenters to execute. Once these
tricks were completed, she could, for example, push a button, which
would make a wall panel recede, and step quickly from one apartment
to another. Then she could open a window and climb out, not on a
roof, but at the top of a flight of steps that would take her down one
story, there to meet another flight that would bring her back up to the
original level. The theory was that this maze of stairs would confuse
the spirits of the Indian ghosts.

In addition to the stairs, she had them build a huge room full of
nothing but balconies of all sorts and sizes. Here the bewildered spirit
might dash around a corner to find that the balcony had suddenly
shrunk from being three feet wide to only three inches. One balcony
led to a door that, once closed, could not be opened again from the
inside, which forced the spirit to find another way to escape.

After at least half an hour of maneuvering, certain that she had
eluded her last ghostly pursuer, Mrs. Winchester would arrive at last in
front of a piece of furniture that resembled a large wardrobe with
drawers in the bottom of it. But it was just another deception, for one
door was not a wardrobe door at all. It really led into the séance room.
Once through this door, she would come out in the secret room on the
other side of the wall. Today, there are spots where the varnish of the
floor was worn away by the constant tread of her slippers. The walls are
painted blue. It is widely believed among superstitious people that this
color frightens away evil spirits. In the room is a cabinet, a comfortable
armchair, and, in front of the latter, a table with paper and pencil for
automatic writing and a planchette board to receive the spirit messages.

Today, there are few people left alive who remember Sarah Winchester. But one of those who does is Maria. Now an old woman
herself, she still shivers about the experience she had as a girl when
she worked in the Winchester House.

It all started quite accidentally. Maria, who had been employed
there for only a month, was hurrying to leave to prepare for a date that
night with a young man. She took a wrong turn as she left the wing of
the house in which she worked. Within a few minutes, she was hopelessly lost in the labyrinth of connecting passages between the (by
then) almost 150 rooms.

At one point she was sure she was near one of the passages to
the outside world; instead, Maria found herself on a stairway of seven
flights. She reached a door and managed to get it open, only to find it
was a false door with a solid wall behind it. Trying desperately to
retrace her steps, she found herself on a sunporch, complete with a
skylight in its floor, that she had never seen. The next room she
entered was also unfamiliar, and she turned to go back out, only to

find that the door to this room did not open from the inside. Finally she found another way out.

Her experience was assuming all the qualities of a nightmare except that it was real. She walked along a balcony and, seeing an open window, stepped through it; but in a moment she found that she was back on another part of the same balcony. By now, she was almost hysterical. On she hurried, up one flight of steps and down another.

Finally, she opened a door and stumbled into a small, windowless cell of a room. There, seated at a table, was a little old lady glaring at her with an expression of terrible rage upon her face. "You have disturbed the spirits," Mrs. Winchester shouted, rising from her chair. It was the first time Maria had ever seen her employer. In fact, Mrs. Winchester was always heavily veiled, and all the servants knew that no one was ever permitted to see her face. The combination of the forbidden sight of her employer's face and the anger she saw there caused the poor girl to faint.

"When I woke up, I was lying on a bed in the servants' quarters and within half an hour was hustled out of the house and driven home. When I got out, the chauffeur gave me an envelope and told me I was not to come to work again. When I opened it, there was my notice from Miss Margaret and six months' salary. But even if I had not been fired, I would never have gone back to that house again."

Were there ghosts or spirits in the Winchester house?

"I really don't know. But one thing I'm sure of is that the spiritualist who said Mrs. Winchester's fortune was haunted by spirits that would harm her was an evil woman. She took advantage of Mrs. Winchester's grief after the death of her husband and told her lies that destroyed her life."

Did anyone ever know who the medium was?

"Only the man who drove her there, I guess, and Miss Margaret must have known, but she didn't have any influence over Mrs. Winchester. It's sad when you think that all Mrs. Winchester's energy and all her money was spent on crazy ways to protect herself from her imaginings."

————————

Mrs. Winchester was convinced by a spiritualistic medium that the lives of her husband and baby daughter had been taken by the spirits of those killed by the "Gun That Won the West." She, too, would share their fate unless she never stopped building a mansion for the spirits. She would live only for as long as she continued to build. She built for almost thirty-eight years. The lavish, 160-room mansion with forty-seven fireplaces, thirteen bathrooms, and endless spiritualistic symbols sprawls over six acres and is a California Historical Landmark. Located at 525 South Winchester Boulevard in San Jose, the house is open daily for tours except on Christmas Day. For more information, telephone (408) 247–2101.

This story is a work of fiction. Names, characters, and events are purely fictitious and a product of the author's imagination. In no way does this story reflect on the present fine management of the Winchester Mystery House, which has been offering guided tours of the sprawling mansion on a daily basis since 1923.

LUCAS TAVERN

Montgomery, Alabama

Old North Hull Street Historic District in Montgomery, Alabama, has a haunted house for a welcome center. How appropriate that it is the home of a ghost said to be unusually cordial. The most frequent accounts of seeing this ghost, the friendly Eliza Lucas, come from people who pass the house at night and see a woman dressed in the style of the early nineteenth century, waving at them from the doorway of the Lucas Tavern. Rather than be rude, most wave back and only begin to wonder about her later, especially if the hour is eleven or twelve at night.

In the 1820s Lucas Tavern offered travelers a comfortable place with clean beds, warm victuals, and a friendly hostess. Undoubtedly one of the great moments of Eliza Lucas's life was when she opened the door to welcome the handsome, bewigged General Lafayette, French hero of the American Revolution, on his visit to Montgomery in 1825. There is no record of what Mrs. Lucas served for dinner that night, but a menu of the tavern fare found later consisted of "chicken pie, ham, five vegetables, pudding and sauce, sweet pies, preserved fruits, a dessert of strawberries and plums, and wine and brandy." All of this cost the traveler only seventy-five cents.

If there are doubters that Eliza's spirit is at the tavern, they may begin to believe after hearing of one Saturday morning in the fall of 1985, when a man arrived, unsolicited, to meet Eliza. He encountered her just inside the front door of the tavern, describing her as of about medium height—about five feet three inches tall—and with a warm, pleasant disposition. Strangely enough the tavern cat, ordinarily very docile, "refuses to go in or out the front door of the tavern unless one of us goes with her, and even then appears uneasy," said Director Mary Ann Neeley. It is a well-known fact that animals often sense the presence of a spirit even when people do not.

The tavern restoration was completed in 1979, and, on January 2, 1980, it became the Visitor's Reception Center and home of the

The old schoolhouse in the Hull Historic District, where the ghostly Eliza once posed for a photographer. (Photo by Bruce Roberts.)

offices for the Historic District. "Soon after we occupied it, Eliza began to make her presence felt," said Ms. Neeley.

"In the winter of 1980, there was a late afternoon meeting in front of the fire in the Tavern Room. The question was controversial, and one person began to speak very heatedly. At that point, a great puff of smoke and ashes erupted from the fireplace, covering the dissident with a coat of chimney soot. All we could think of was that Eliza had not agreed with the speaker and expressed herself forcefully.

"On another occasion two staff members were sitting at a table having lunch and were discussing the Historic District and its operation. With no warning, the door to the room began to just slide off its hinges. As they watched, it continued to slide and then struck the floor with a resounding thud. Again, Eliza had manifested her displeasure over something that had been said.

"Objects disappear, only to reappear in new locations. Eliza rearranges, straightens, messes things up, or leaves them about in a quite unpredictable fashion. Nor can we be sure where she will reappear next."

The back door of the Lucas Tavern opens onto a square containing several buildings of the 1800–1898 period. The Hull restoration brings the nineteenth century to life and is highly popular with visitors, some of whom are amateur photographers. Vincent Ives was one of them. He enjoys showing his vacation slides to family and friends. In the late summer of 1986, he coaxed a hostess into letting him stay to shoot some pictures after the restoration was closed for the day.

When the last visitor had left, and the tour guides as well, Vincent went out through the Lucas Tavern's back door and into the square with the other nineteenth-century buildings. They were bathed in the wonderful, warm light of late afternoon. He knew it would not last long, and he moved quickly from one building to another, shooting.

The third buiding was the 1890 schoolhouse, which was one of his favorites. It was filled with all the materials a student would have found in a classroom of the 1800s. Earlier he had noticed all the wonderful details there. There was the pot-bellied little stove, the old pine schoolmaster desk, the kerosene lamp, the abacus, and the slates. It would have been nice to leave this building until last, like a dessert, but the light inside the schoolroom would be going soon, and he did not want to use a flash.

Vincent started toward the schoolhouse, thinking he might want to place some "school days" objects on the windowsill for a still arrangement. It would be great to have a teacher to photograph in there or someone using a slate or abacus, but that was out of the question. He had a sense of awe as he thought about all the boys and girls who had sat at these desks long ago, students who had grown up and left their mark in the world but who had now been gone for many more years than he had even been alive.

Closing the door quietly behind him, he looked around the room to decide where he would begin first. Then he started in surprise. All of the guides must not have gone, for there sat one in her nineteenth-century costume. She could be a picture subject for him, perhaps pose as the teacher. She was over near the window and seemed absorbed in a book with a blue cover. Why had she stayed on after all the others had left?

It didn't really matter, though, for in that old-fashioned dress, with the light coming from the window beside her, she would make a great picture. Vincent started to ask her permission and then thought how ridiculous that was because none of the guides minded having their pictures taken. Besides, she might change position, and she was perfect just the way she was. Very quietly and unobtrusively he began to shoot, moving a little to this side or that, adjusting the lens, bracketing. Unfortunately, the tripod he was carrying struck the leg of a desk a sharp crack, and the sound seemed to startle her. Hurriedly, she got up to leave.

"Wait! Don't go, please. I wonder if I could shoot a picture or two of you there at the old schoolmaster desk? It won't take long." She did not reply, which seemed rude, and, instead of going toward the desk to sit down, she stopped under the picture of George Washington.

Oh, no, thought Vincent. He might be able to get her to pose there under the portrait, but it was too high to show over her head. The picture of her sitting at the desk absorbed in the book would have looked much more natural, as it really might have come from out of the past.

"Pardon me, ma'am. I'm Vincent . . . . " Then his heart began to pound and his lips refused to form the words he was about to say. As he stood there in the middle of the schoolroom, ready to coax his subject into sitting over at the desk, she reached the picture of Washington. For the first time she appeared to acknowledge Vincent's presence, and she turned to wave at him slowly and deliberately. The eyes in the face never really seemed to react to him as a person, although they appeared to stare directly at his face. It was a warm August day in Montgomery, but as Vincent looked back at her, he felt chilled to the bone. Then, to his great astonishment, she simply floated right through the wall beneath George Washington's portrait as effortlessly if she were passing through a door.

"Ma'am, ma'am . . .," he called out weakly, as if to summon her back. But words failed him, and he sat down in the front row of desks and stared at the area under the portrait. Then he arose and, walking over to the portrait, ran his fingers over the wall beneath it as he searched for some sign of a door or of a secret panel that would press inward. He couldn't accept the fact that she had disappeared. It was almost dark outside when he finally decided to leave. A little dizzy and with his knees still a bit weak, Vincent walked over to the desk where she had been sitting. On it was an abacus that looked as if it were being used for sums. The blue book she had been holding was a McGuffey Reader, written in the mid-1800s for children.

The next day he asked one of the guides if Eliza was ever seen in other places besides the front of the tavern.

"Her spirit you mean? Oh, my goodness, yes. She's a lively one, if you will pardon the pun. She has been seen in many different buildings here at the restoration, often the schoolhouse. I doubt if she was ever able to get much formal education in her time, coming from a humble background. But if there was ever anyone who probably would have wanted to better herself, it was Eliza Lucas. She was an ambitious woman and a hard worker."

"We all feel Eliza's presence without question, and, even while I talk about her now, I somehow feel she is trying to tell me how I should present her story," said Ms. Neeley. "The question is why does Eliza's spirit continue to visit the tavern? My own feeling is that, having lived and operated the tavern for more than twenty years, she probably found her most fulfilling moments in this building. It was here that she reared her family and was recognized far and wide as a hostess. We are very fond of Eliza, and I believe she is of us.

"I'll bet she's around here somewhere right now. Wouldn't it be something if you could get a picture of her! Why, Mr. Ives, you look white as a sheet. Are you feeling all right?"

"Yes, of course."

"Mr. Ives, what is that book at your feet?"

Vincent leaned down, and, as he looked at the book, his heart began beating madly. It was the McGuffey Reader. He read the child's name on the flyleaf, the same name he had seen a few minutes ago on the reader in the schoolhouse! How did it get here? It was almost as if she were giving him her "calling card."

"A book on the floor, eh? That's our Eliza, at it again. Did you get some good pictures?"

"I hope so."

"Do come back and see us, Mr. Ives. We want to welcome you just as Eliza would have done if she were here."

As soon as he returned to his car, he unloaded the film he had shot in the schoolroom and marked the top of the can "Eliza." He sent the roll off to Kodak when he returned home, not trusting it to a local processor. When he picked it up and put the slides on his lightbox, the pictures of the buildings were fine, as were those of the exterior of the schoolhouse.

But all the frames he had shot inside were blank except for showing a streak of bright, golden light over at the left or the middle or the right, never in the same place, but "depending on where 'Eliza' was standing as I moved around framing my picture," he said to himself wonderingly as he looked at his slides. He smiled. All he needed to do now was to find a photography book with instructions for the proper exposure to capture both a ghost and the man-made backdrop of a schoolroom.

———————

The Lucas Tavern is in the Old North Hull Street Historic District, open Monday through Saturday from 9:30 A.M. to 4 P.M. and Sunday from 1:30 P.M. to 3:30 P.M. Admission is charged. For more information, write 310 North Hull Street, Montgomery, Alabama 36104 or telephone (205) 262-0322.

WHALEY HOUSE (MUSEUM)

San Diego, California

The Whaley House in San Diego is one of only two houses in California that the United States Chamber of Commerce has authenticated as being genuinely haunted. What does "genuinely haunted" mean? Let's visit San Diego's "Old Town" and find out. If you prefer not to go, however, you will surely miss all the atmosphere of old San Diego, seeing the oldest house in the city—and, perhaps, one of the ghosts.

Sipping a cool drink at the Crazy Gringo Restaurant in Old Town, I was fortunate enough to be listening to the story of a pleasant, gray-haired lady who has known and loved The Whaley House for more than a quarter of a century. June Reading, graduate of the University of Minnesota, is curator and chief historian. She undoubtedly has done more research and knows more than anyone else in the world about the Whaley family and their house north of downtown San Diego. Of course, it is a historic site now, which people come to visit from all over the world. No members of the Whaley family inhabit the house anymore. At least none that are still alive.

Whaley House has been written about in many publications, and, if you have been wondering as you read these stories what makes a house haunted, a description by D. Scott Rogo, author of *In Search of the Unknown*, may enlighten you. It seems to describe this house particularly.

Whaley House has witnessed more history than other houses in Old Town. Its uses have been many. It has served not only as a home but as city hall, Protestant church and Sunday school, public school, U.S. Post Office, Polls Theatre, county seat of government, and community social center.

Rogo says that what is necessary are apparitions, unaccountable cold feelings or sensations of being touched by something intangible, and other phenomena such as lights, footsteps, rappings, movements of objects, unaccountable odors, and presences. June Reading says that

Supernatural happenings are not "out of the ordinary" at the Whaley House, San Diego's oldest home. It is one of two houses that the state has authenticated as haunted.

Whaley House has exhibited all of these phenomena and more since 1960, the year it was opened to the public. From then to the present, "the manifestations are still going on."

Mrs. Reading was "in on the ground floor," we might say, since she was active from the very beginning of the restoration of the house. The first events she remembers occurred during the early work on the house, and I found myself listening for something later as we stood looking around the narrow downstairs hall.

"One day in the spring of 1960, I had come over here early, intending to see about furnishing the upstairs rooms. Two staff members from the San Diego Historical Society were loaned to me to help with the delivery of the furniture and other items. As I walked to the back door, they followed. When I reached up to unbolt the door, we heard the sound of walking, of what sounded like a large person wearing boots striding across the upper floor. My companions insisted that someone else was in the house, so I mounted the stairs and called out, hoping to get a response—to no avail. As I turned to come down, saying 'There's no one upstairs,' they both looked at each other and said, 'Well, maybe Thomas Whaley's come back to look the place over!'

Suddenly, we heard the sound of footsteps coming from the bedroom above us. It was just as if someone were walking about up there in heavy boots. We started up the stairs. I thought another workman had arrived ahead of us, but when I came up here to see, no one was up here.

"'Who is upstairs?' asked one of the men. I shook my head, and he laughed about spirits coming back to look things over, and I thought no more about it. We were so busy getting the house ready to open to the public. But in the days after it was opened, I would often hear the footsteps and find myself going upstairs again and again, sure that someone must be up there. Sometimes it happened when I was busy at my desk downstairs or when visitors were on the lower floor. I would sit at my desk and hear footsteps descend the hall stairs, but they always stopped about three steps from the bottom.

"One morning, in October of 1962, I was giving a talk to twenty-five schoolchildren who were touring the house. This time the sound of footsteps began to come from the flat roof. The schoolchildren began to look up at the ceiling curiously and ask who was making the noise, so I went outside to see if it was a repairman sent by the county. No one was up there. When I mentioned some of these events to people in the neighborhood, they told me this sort of phenomenon had gone on for years."

The last member of the family to live in the house had been Lillian Whaley. She was well aware that unusual things went on there, and, during the many years she lived in the house, she had complained. On one occasion she even told of a heavy china cabinet that, without cause, suddenly toppled over. That was in 1912, one year before Frank Whaley's death. Lillian Whaley lived all her life in Whaley House and was the only child who did not marry. She died in 1953 at the age of 89.

On one occasion while Mrs. Reading was guiding a tour, a woman visitor complained that she had felt unseen hands pushing her out of an upstairs bedroom. And many who have come to the house mention their smelling the fragrance of cologne, rosewater, or the aroma of cigar smoke when they have been alone in one of the rooms.

One such tourist, Mrs. Kirby, wife of the director of the Medical Association of New Westminster, British Columbia, was convinced that she had seen the apparition of a woman in the house's courtroom. She described a small, olive-skinned lady in a bright calico dress with a full skirt down to the floor who simply "stared through me."

Among the ghosts who, I am told, have been seen in the house with regularity is Squire Augustus S. Ensworth, an attorney who managed Thomas Whaley's business enterprises in San Diego while Whaley was in military service in the Quartermaster Department and Commissary of Subsistence in San Francisco during the Civil War. Squire Ensworth died before the battle over the county seat. He was very fond of the Whaley House and took great pride in keeping it in good repair during Mr. Whaley's absence. Ensworth wrote about 200 letters to Whaley telling him news of the community, weather reports, and about his house and business. We believe Augustus Ensworth's spirit still hovers around Whaley House; he was a very charming, knowledgeable gentleman. Mrs. Anna Whaley is presumably responsible for the occasional snatches of piano music. And then there is the spirit of a small child, little Tom Whaley, who died in one of the upstairs rooms when only seventeen months old.

The eerie events that have happened to guides in the house and to tourists as well do not happen every day. Sometimes weeks go by, and nothing out of the ordinary occurs, nothing, that is, that would send chills down one's spine or cause one to shiver in this house on a warm day. But then something will take place that no one can explain. June Reading tells the story of such an event.

"In the early 1980s, a lovely college girl named Denise Pournelle worked at the house during the summer, and, from the moment she arrived, she went around telling everyone how she would love to see a ghost. Things like this can be dangerous to say, particularly in certain houses where even the walls may be listening. I always thought it was like tempting providence, but Denise kept right on. I talked with her and advised her to be patient.

"'Denise, sooner or later you are going to hear walking, you are going to hear music, you will even get the feeling that someone is touching you. You will have all kinds of things happen to you.' Of course, I was right.

"It was during Christmas vacation, and she was like a child loving to dress up in costume. We always did that here at the house on special occasions. That afternoon we were all in our old-fashioned long dresses. There was a cold rain most of the day, and we had very few visitors except for one little boy. This boy walked about the house trying to hear the sound of a ghost. He also sat on the stairs, thinking that, if he concentrated, he might hear footsteps. The kids that come here are so cute. I remember him because he had a pair of tennis shoes on that were very, very clean.

"The hostesses were sitting around because there was so little activity. I hadn't eaten anything, and it was getting into the afternoon, so I told them I was going out to have a late lunch. When I came back, they were all waiting for me at the door. Before I could even get my coat off, they said, 'While you were gone, we heard the footsteps upstairs, not once but twice. There was a long pause, and then they started again.'

"Denise's dark eyes were sparkling, and her pretty face was filled with excitement, so I said, 'Denise, why don't you come upstairs with me? I'm a little suspicious.' I had that little boy with the tennis shoes on my mind instead of any ghost, because that child could have slipped away from the ladies without their noticing it and gone up-stairs into one of the rooms.

"Denise picked up her long skirt, and up we went. The first place we walked into was the master bedroom, and two windows were standing wide open. It was pouring rain, and the rain had come in and was all over the floor, and the curtains were dripping wet. I was angry and said to myself, do you suppose that boy came up here and opened those windows and prowled around?

"Together, we looked in the other rooms but could see no evi-dence that anyone had been in them. The rain was so bad that it was almost dark out, although it was only about two-thirty in the after-noon. So I began to close the windows, but the frames are all the original white cedar that swells up just like a sponge when it gets wet. They were so swollen that I could hardly close them, and I certainly don't know how anyone could have pulled them open.

"I could not get them bolted, and I said, 'Denise, you are going to have to go downstairs and get a hammer.' She said, 'Let me try it,' and together we finally got the bolt over. Then we walked over to the nursery and, once there, began to relax because nothing was out of place. Suddenly, just a few feet behind us, a man's deep laugh rang out. Denise said, 'Did you hear that?' I said, 'What did you hear?' She said, 'I heard a man's laughter.' I said, 'So did I!' She: 'Let's get out of here!' and with that, she picked up her skirts, down the stairs she went—lickety out—dashed to the telephone and called her mother. I knew that in that afternoon we had both heard laughter from the past—very probably the baritone laughter of Thomas Whaley. I felt what I can describe only as an intense electric shock go the length of my back, and for a few seconds I stood there frozen, truly unable to move. I have never had anything affect me like that.

"As for Denise, her face was white and her eyes, terrified. She shot out of the room and in an instant reached the top of the stairs. Down we went, more quickly than I would ever have imagined we could with those long dresses. It is a wonder we didn't break our necks. I don't recall Denise ever mentioning any desire for a supernatural experience again.

"After we began to talk about it downstairs, I remembered that the place where we had been standing when we heard the laugh was right over the location of the old gallows that stood there before Thomas Whaley built this house. He had watched the hanging of a colorful man named 'Yankee Jim.' Imprisoned for attempting to steal a boat, Yankee Jim's crime does not seem as grave as the sort for which men were ordinarily sentenced to hang. Unfortunately for him, his trial came upon the heels of the Indian uprising of 1851, when San

Diego had been under martial law and any sort of disorder occasioned swift and sometimes harsh action.

"Yankee Jim did not take the sentence to hang him seriously, and, believing he would be pardoned at the last minute, even made jokes on his way to the gallows. But he was not pardoned. His last moments were painful indeed, for, when the wagon in which he was standing was pulled from under his feet, his neck remained unbroken. He continued to live for almost an hour, until he finally strangled to death."

Is it possible that the laugh they heard that afternoon was Yankee Jim? "It may have been," admitted Mrs. Reading. "I wonder, sometimes, if certain sounds remain in the atmosphere, and now and then something we do sets them off, and we hear that sound again exactly as it once occurred. The footsteps, the laugh, even the old-fashioned melodies we occasionally hear playing in the music room of the house . . . Thomas Whaley once wrote in a letter to his mother, 'My wife is the best little woman in the world, loved by all, she is proficient in music, plays and sings.'

"I could tell you many strange things, but the sound of that deep laugh shocked me more than anything else that has ever happened to me in this house. An event occurred just before Christmas, when several of us were in the old courtroom getting popcorn and cranberry ropes and other old-fashioned ornaments ready for the tree. One of the hostesses very quietly went around to get a good view and shot a picture of all of us. After the film had been sent off and developed, she brought in the prints. To her own and everyone else's amazement, over at the edge of the group stood a woman in a period dress. The resemblance to Mrs. Whaley is striking."

The story Mrs. Reading told about Thomas Whaley's career in the early days of California was so interesting that I wanted her to finish it after I had interviewed her about the reputation the house has for ghosts. Not only is she director of Whaley House, but she is the author of a booklet on its history.

June Reading's colorful anecdotes about people and her descriptions of early San Diego gave me the feeling that she was talking about something contemporary. It was almost like living in two time frames simultaneously, and I kept thinking that she was telling me something that had just happened.

Mrs. Reading has been associated with the house since the late 1950s, when it was purchased by San Diego County and began to be restored by the Historical Shrine Foundation. She has done many years of research and says, "I am still doing it. Scarcely a month passes that I don't discover something new." Some of her most productive research trips have been to Sitka, Alaska, where Thomas Whaley was once appointed commissary storekeeper and took possession of the Alaska Territory for the United States. At that time his wife, Anna, and their children stayed in San Francisco with friends.

Whaley had engaged Augustus S. Ensworth as a partner by then, and Ensworth was tending to the former's business affairs in San Diego. When the family moved back there, the house was remodeled to accommodate more children. Lillian Whaley was only three years old when the family returned to San Diego in 1867. This is a portion of what she wrote regarding their return:

"We were taken to that big room, afterwards used as the court-room . . . . My father was altering the other portion of the house at the time. My next recollection is of being awakened by Father Ubach's ringing the Angelus at six o'clock in the morning. Father was putting in a lath-and-plaster partition, making a hallway through the center of the house. The whole front was open. The arch that stands between the parlors was in place. It is said that Yankee Jim, who had been arrested for stealing a boat, was hanged over the spot."

After the courtroom had been in use for some time, a sharp controversy was instigated by New Town (San Diego) and Old Town for the county seat. Threats were made to remove the records, and they almost erupted into violence. Thomas Whaley, feeling that all was temporarily quiet and secure, went to San Francisco on business. Within a few hours after he had left, the opposition, led by County Clerk Chalmers Scott lost no time. On the night of March 31, 1871, Scott and his armed party took two wagons, their wheels muffled by gunny sacks, over to the Whaley House and knocked on the door.

Lillian Whaley, youngest of the children, jumped out of bed, thinking her father had arrived home. When she ran out in the hall to greet him, she found her tiny, four-foot eleven-inch mother surrounded by armed men. When Whaley returned home and discovered that his wife had been threatened and the records removed, he was furious. The lease on the courtroom was not up, and, until the end of his life, he continued to write angry letters to the county demanding rent and repairs for the damage to the building caused by the break-in. These were never acknowledged, and his requests that the action be reviewed were denied.

Thus the archives of San Diego County had been taken from the oldest city in California to its brash and lusty young neighbor, and the glory of Old Town was gone. Thomas Whaley died in 1890; and the old house, many-hued in its ruins, looked out over a San Diego Street deserted by all but specters of the past. Its uniquely classical architecture spoke of the way of life of a century ago. In the 1950s a decision was made by the county to purchase the house, and it was afterward restored.

For those who are fascinated by ghost stories, it is said that four different ghosts have been identified at the Whaley House. The most noisy is reputed to be that of the legendary Yankee Jim.

———————————

Whatever your tastes, you are welcome to enjoy a tour of this early home of the Old West. Located at 2482 San Diego Avenue in Old Town, San Diego, California, Whaley House, with its rich and violent chronicles of yesteryear, is now open to the public year-round, Wednesday through Sunday. For more information, telephone (619) 298-2482. For those who suffer from the summer heat elsewhere, cool breezes off the bay and temperatures during the day ranging between 65 and 75 degrees are delightful. Bring a sweater for evenings outdoors.

THE ROW HOUSE

San Francisco, California

"I looked for about a year before I found this Queen Anne row house," said our host, Maurice. We were in the heart of San Francisco, not far from Market Street. "I wanted something that had lots of space and two main levels and an attic," he continued. "This house immediately attracted me. It had such close proximity to downtown, and, although it was built in 1903, structurally it was in great condition. The woodwork was beautiful, as were the moldings around the doors and the medallions in the ceilings. When I first moved in, I began to paint the complete interior just to make it more livable until I decorated."

What was the first unusual thing that Maurice noticed?

"It actually happened the first time I walked up the stairway. When I came in to look at the house, as soon as I set foot on this level, I looked around and got this funny sort of feeling. I didn't know what it was, but it was as if someone was speaking to me. It was a woman's voice, and she was saying. 'This is your house; welcome.' I was so surprised, for I thought it might be the realtor, and then I realized she had suggested I go on up while she checked the sheet on the house in her book. I was alone. But somehow the voice was more friendly than frightening.

"After looking all over the house, I was ready to buy it. I thought it would be just a matter of signing and having the closing, but it didn't work that way. There were many hurdles, and, due to the problems that came up, negotiations went on for a year. But I kept hearing that voice I heard when I first walked up here. From the time I moved in, I always felt sort of a presence back by the old stairway and over toward the kitchen. A well-known psychic from Los Angeles came to the house. You may have seen the feature on her in the *National Enquirer*. Her name is Clarissa.

"She confirmed that what I had experienced was right. I told her I thought it was a woman. It felt like the presence of an elderly

116

The owner felt a presence in this Victorian row house when it was first shown to him by a realtor.

woman, but I never saw her." He stopped in the hallway just outside the kitchen and looked around him. "This is where I have felt her presence. Somewhere right along here," he said, standing a few feet from the top of the stairs.

Does Maurice ever feel this presence while he is cooking in the kitchen?

"No, normally just when I pass through this hall or, perhaps, come up the stairs and reach the top. Clarissa told me that the lady was always walking over to the stairway to greet people or wait for someone. It was as if she were saying, 'Welcome.' She was a ballet teacher, and her daughter was a ballet dancer. They were both very involved with the arts.

"This is a strange building. It was built, I am almost positive, for the sole purpose of providing the work area downstairs. The man who lived in the small building next door was a carriage builder. My garage was once his shop, and he worked there, building carriages until late at night. There was a sliding barn door that he rolled his carriages through when he had completed them. The psychic was convinced that she felt the presence of this man and said that he was a hard worker, and he and his wife didn't get along. But the only one that I am really sensitive to is the lady in the hall."

As we sat in the small, peaceful garden in the San Francisco morning sunlight, it was hard to think about ghosts. Attractive flower beds were edged with succulents, and blue agapanthus were in bloom against a backdrop of ferns and native plants. Two pumps kept a small stream flowing through the garden, and goldfish swam languidly past. As I left, I looked back at the house, one of many Victorian row houses, but it would never be exactly like all the others because it was the only one with the presence of a ballet teacher out of the past.

This home in San Francisco is privately owned and not available for tours.

BACON'S CASTLE

Surry, Virginia

Across the river from Jamestown, Virginia, the south shore rises in a vast, green plateau remarkable mainly for its flatness. Beyond it lie the emerald fields of Surry County. It was there in Surry, along the James River, that the region's first houses of grace and size were built.

A few miles away, young John Harrison of Berkeley Plantation must have watched in amazement while the largest and most elaborate house in Virginia took shape. Rising above its full basement, it grew a full two stories high and was capped by a steep-roofed attic. The house, still standing today, is Jacobean with the features of Tudor England. Its outside chimneys are like three grouped stacks, and projecting from both front and rear are towers of porches and stairs. Within are impressive, timbered ceilings constructed of double-crossed girders. Called Bacon's Castle because, in 1676, it was held and fortified by the colorful rebel Nathaniel Bacon, the house is a gem in a setting of holly and magnolia trees. It stands out today, as it did then, like some ancient castle dominating the flatland. But only a few know that it is the site of a most eerie phenomenon.

In the late summer of 1863, the owners of the great plantations had yet to taste the bitter anguish that the Civil War would bring to most of them. For a few golden months, life for the John Hankins family, including daughter Virginia, was as happy and comfortable as it had always been. There was the vast farm to supervise, servants to do most of the heavy work, and some luxuries for the table. The hardships of the war were not really felt.

It was a warm Friday night in July, shortly after midnight, when Virginia Hankins was awakened by the sound of horses' hooves and men's voices. She hurried to the window and saw a group of soldiers in front of the house. Were they Yankees? Confederates? Or worst of all, were they bummers—the riffraff of both armies? Just as she was becoming fearful, she saw one of them step forward into a circle of moonlight

119

Bacon's Castle, scene of the ill-fated romance of Virginia Hankins and Sidney Lanier. An unusual phenomenon has taken place here ever since. (Photo by Bruce Roberts.)

and raise a flute to his lips. It was a Confederate soldier, and the flute's romantic notes reverberated in the warm July night.

Ginna smiled delightedly. With seven brothers she could be certain that the serenade was meant for her alone. On and on went the melody, and the girl marveled at its beauty. Nor is it any wonder that she was charmed, for this was no common soldier-troubador but rather a young man who was later called the most accomplished flutist in America, his music described as "weird, mysterious, and entrancing." In the midst of his serenade came a crash of thunder followed by a downpour of rain. The soldiers clambered upon their horses and galloped away.

Next morning Ginna found a torn piece of paper tied to the front door with a guitar string. Upon it was written:

> Porch, Saturday morning, 1 o'clock.
> Did all that mortal men could to serenade you—
> failure owing entirely to inclemency of the weather.
> Field Corps.

The following afternoon three young Confederate scouts galloped up to the house with a flurry and introduced themselves to Mr. Hankins and the rest of the family. They were from the state of Georgia, and their ringleader was Sidney Lanier, a young man who was later to become one of the South's most famous poets. The other two soldiers were his brother, Clifford, and a good friend, Will Hopson. Soon the threesome and the Hankins family were friends.

The three soldiers were guests at the house often, for it was close to Fort Boykin, where the scouts were stationed, and the Hankins table was a real contrast to camp fare. The young Confederates enjoyed luxuries like Virginia biscuits, spring chickens, and ham and eggs, and, when they spent the night at Bacon's Castle, mint juleps were served before they were out of bed. Sidney regaled Ginna with exciting stories of brushes with the enemy, moonlight dashes down the beach near Hampton Roads, and occasionally about events he had been through at Petersburg. Although it was rare that he spoke of the fighting there, he happened to do so on one of the first afternoons they had a real opportunity to talk. A comrade for whom he had great affection had been killed at his side, and he could not put it out of his mind.

With tears in her eyes, Ginna placed a hand gently on his and quoted from the poet Shelley's famous "Adonais."

He has outsoared the shadow of our night.
Envy and hate and calumny and that unrest
    which men miscall delight,
shall touch him not nor torture not again.

Sidney, a budding poet, was astonished and delighted to find that Ginna was familiar with Shelley; from then on, he began to read his own poetry to her. Ginna was well educated and able to appreciate and discuss the poems intelligently with him. At the time, he was working on his novel, *Tiger Lilies*, but from that moment on the only literary works completed by Sidney were the love poems he addressed to Ginna.

Together they read the work of writers she had never known before and paced the long galleries of her home discussing books and ideas. Lanier quoted feelingly the poems of Schiller and Goethe while a rapturous Ginna listened. They delighted in sharing poetry and literature, and the time Sidney was stationed at Fort Boykin sped by.

It was during these months that Lanier composed an unusually beautiful poem to Ginna, calling her his "Most Rare Brown Bird on Eden's Tree and All Heaven Sweet to Me."

He wrote of her later to their mutual friend, Hopson, confessing, "Ginna H. and I have become firm soul-friends . . . I've initiated her into the beauties of Mrs. Browning and Robert B., together with Carlyle and Novalis; . . . she is in a perfect blaze of enthusiasm." Can any couple share the Brownings' romantic poetry together and remain only friends? The first verse of one of Browning's poems may answer that question.

So Boyhood sets; comes Youth,
A painful night of mists and dreams,
   That broods, till Love's exquisite truth,
The star of a morn-clear manhood, beams!

For Sidney, 1863 and early 1864 was one of those interludes of gaiety between battles, a highly charged atmosphere of love, music, and literature, but an interlude that could not last. Perhaps his and Ginna's future was predicted in that poem of Mrs. Browning called "Drama of Exile," which the couple read together. But who can see the future when the moment contains such happiness?

If we had been at Bacon's Castle that fall, we might have looked out the window and watched them often riding away on horseback from this huge, rambling house and off into the green woods of the estate, she on the sorrel stallion and Lanier, a tall, thin, dramatic figure, on the large white bay. As they rode among the trees of the forest, brilliant with its crimson and gold autumn leaves, and through amber patches of sunlight, riders and mounts must have made an idyllic picture.

Often the pair emerged from the woods laughing and talking. Then they would canter across fields purple with flowers and down to the river. Wherever the morning mist parted and the sun's rays struck it, the waters of the James sparkled and shimmered. On the well-worn trail beside the water, the horses frequently would break into a gallop. The girl rode slightly ahead, her long brown hair floating out around her.

When they came back to the house, they would sometimes rein in their horses beside Old Brick Church near the cemetery. Here they would dismount and sit talking on the steps of the church until, with reluctance, young Lanier would help her gently back upon her horse, and together they would return to the house.

Does this sound too much like romantic fiction? Perhaps, to some of us today. But there are people who are fortunate enough to possess experiences worth treasuring, and that is the way it was in the lives of Ginna Hankins of Bacon's Castle and Sidney Lanier. Both were unusually talented. Ginna, too, wrote poetry, and Lanier not only had poetic and musical genius but, in the military world of hard riding and dangerous living, "a cool and collected courage."

For those who may be envious, there must at least be some vicarious pleasure in knowing that love or beauty, even in the life of another, is cause for hope and celebration. Certainly Sidney and Ginna, his "Little Brown Bird," would have agreed.

All of this, however, was suddenly interrupted. In August of 1864, Lanier and four other scouts were ordered to report to the heroic Major General William Whiting at Wilmington, North Carolina.

Old Brick Church, where Ginna and Sidney often rested from their horseback rides, is now in ruins. Sometimes the peculiar manifestation is seen near the ruins. (Photo by Bruce Roberts.)

Their assignment was the hazardous duty of serving as signal officers on blockade runners at the last port the bloody and beleaguered South had been able to hold.

Sidney and Ginna said good-byes that were to be for a short time only, until he could get back to Bacon's Castle for their marriage. Her letters, both loving and merry, followed him, but one was to change their future tragically, for with it came the news that Mrs. Hankins had died, leaving a grief-stricken husband and seven young sons at Bacon's Castle.

To Ginna, duty was clear. She believed her first responsibility was to take care of her father and bring up seven little brothers. Sadly but firmly she rejected Sidney's proposal, convinced that marriage was now out of the question. In December of 1867 Lanier married, but he and Ginna continued to correspond for the rest of his life. Their correspondence to each other was in the form of poems.

In the years after the war, Ginna no longer had enough money to keep up Bacon's Castle. Its immense acreage lay idle. Where was the cash to pay for labor to cultivate crops, and where were the hands to harvest them?

Lincoln's assassination was the death of Southerners' hopes to resurrect their wrecked plantations and their lives, for soon a bayonet-supported occupation government arrived in Virginia to feed on a dead society. Controlling the tax bureaus, the officials sent out decla-

The window of Bacon's Castle mentioned by eyewitnesses to the event. (Photo by Bruce Roberts.)

rations that plantations owed tremendous back taxes for the four years of the war. Then they either seized them or forced their owners to sell.

Ginna sold Bacon's Castle for only fifty-five cents an acre, or six thousand dollars, but, paltry sum though it was, it at least bought food and shelter for herself and her brothers. Not long after her death, the phenomenon which is still occurring at Bacon's Castle was seen for the first time.

Frances Richardson has shown visitors through the house for the past six years and is a native of the area. "I have heard all my life that Bacon's Castle had a ghost. The light is said to start sometimes at a certain large tree near the house, make its way to the Old Brick Church Cemetery, encircle it, and slowly come back to the house. Finally, it goes in the window at the west end of the garret, and no one sees it come out.

"My parents and grandparents before them saw it. The light has also been reported by visitors. Of course, scientists try to explain it. They say it is atmospheric conditions, but I'm not so sure . . ."

Like the Richardson family, other people who live near the house have no real explanation for the light, either. They know only that it has been seen for more than a century, and romantics among them equate it with Sidney Lanier's "Little Brown Bird," the lovely Ginna.

A tourist couple who visited the house recently said, "We had stayed at Bacon's Castle until almost dusk, and then we decided to walk around the grounds for a while. Before we knew it, the sun had gone down, and it was dark."

It was then that Brian Butler looked back at the house. "Good heavens! What in the world is that, Eleanor?"

"What is what?"

"Look up in the sky toward the house."

"It's the moon—it's a plane on fire—it's . . ."

"You don't know what it is any more than I do."

"It's a ball of yellow light."

"And it's coming down toward us!"

The couple ran to the shelter of the trees, but the light wasn't really following them. It was headed slowly in the direction of the ruins of Old Brick Church. As they watched, the ball of light circled the church and floated back to Bacon's Castle. When it reached the house it rose in the air and entered the window at the direct west end of the garret.

Although the Butlers waited for what they claimed was at least fifteen minutes, the light did not come out of the house. This was in the fall of 1986, and, strangely enough, other tourists reported seeing this light, which natives of the area, like the Richardsons, have known about for years.

Scientists attribute the light to "simply atmospheric conditions," but others tell a different story. They say it is the spirit of the lovely Ginna Hankins going to the church where she and her sweetheart lingered so often, the church that would have been the scene of her wedding. Ginna, in one of her letters to Sidney long after his marriage, reminisced about the "days we spent cavorting through the purple fields of Surry and along the banks of the sparkling James."

Has the love of this young woman for the dashing Georgia poet survived her earthly body? In any event, there is something bright and luminous, something startling and inexplicable, that has appeared at Bacon's Castle over the years that science has never satisfactorily resolved.

Bacon's Castle, on Highway 617, one mile off Highway 10 at Surry, Virginia, is open daily to the public. For hours and information, telephone (804) 357-5976 or write to Bacon's Castle, Surry, Virginia 23883.

THE HOUSE ON CHURCH STREET

Charleston, South Carolina

Why do we decide to make a phone call at a certain time? Why are we impelled to turn down one street instead of another? Is not only our character but every small act and decision programmed into us years or even eons ago? I cannot tell you why, of all the Charleston houses shrouded in ghost lore, only one attracted me strongly on the day after Thanksgiving in November of 1985. As I write this, I feel some mysterious affinity with a young man who arrived in this city two centuries ago, in 1786.

Before I left on a research trip to the South Carolina Low Country, I looked over a book entitled *60 Famous Houses of Charleston*, a collection of stories done in the late 1960s about historically important residences. I decided that the house I would probably research was the one on Church Street.

Church Street is one-way, and the first time I turned on it, I had gone too far. I made a circle and tried again. Yes, there was the house, a beautiful old two-story home built about 1732 and maintained perfectly. This time I was able to park almost in front. As I sat in the car trying to decide what to do next, I noticed two men going into the garden, and they left the gate ajar. It was an opportunity to see one of the beautiful gardens that many Charleston homes have, gardens so often hidden by brick walls. Admiring a ribbon of flaming scarlet azaleas, I spoke to the men whose strong, brown hands were expertly weeding, raking, and trimming back the plants.

"The garden is lovely. I imagine the mistress of the house tells you just what to do, doesn't she?"

"No'm. She let me pretty much do it my way," said the older man proudly. One of the carriages filled with tourists creaked and clattered past, and I heard the guide's voice with its practiced patter relate a spattering of history.

The tree-lined street was quiet now and, for the moment, deserted. All sense of time seemed to fade. My mind flashed back to the

Sometimes the two elderly ladies would hear the sound of a merry whistle on the stairway just as they did when the doctor was alive. The jogging board used by the little girl is still on the piazza.

people who lived here two hundred years ago, when a handsome, brown-haired young man looked down Church Street just as I was doing now.

It was early in 1786, during a storm with its winter wind coming in from the sea, when young Joseph Ladd Brown arrived from Rhode Island in this city where he was to spend the rest of his all-too-brief life. He had come to Charleston, often called the London of the New World, to practice medicine and pen the verses he loved to write.

The driver flung open the door of the coach in front of a small, waterfront tavern. He was eager to rid himself of his passenger on this miserable night and feel the warmth of a hot toddy in his gullet.

"Here ye be. Couldn't find no better place to lodge than the Red Lion, sir." And with that he took Brown by the arm and, half supporting, half tugging, assisted his passenger from the coach. Doctor Brown's relief upon entering the warm tavern was momentary, for he was quick to note that the crowd within was a rowdy one.

Although the curtain had gone down officially on the age of pirates, their breed had not disappeared. There were men all around Joseph who looked to be the hoodlums and scum of the sea. Some had knives or pistols thrust menacingly in their belts or barely concealed. Others had faces wickedly scarred, an eye gone, or a leg missing. Their clothing, wet from the weather outside and warmed by the heat from the blazing fireplace, gave off a most revolting stench.

Exhausted as he was from his ride, the doctor became instantly alert. He had no desire to be the epitome of fashion, but his expensive boots imported from England, his beaver-fur hat, and the fine-quality fabric and tailoring of his coat were making him the subject of envious, speculative glances. He knew he was in a dangerous situation, which would become more so if some of the men realized he was alone and strange to the city.

As Joseph looked about with growing apprehension, the door of the tavern opened and a well-dressed man entered and called out to the tavernkeeper. "I am looking for one of my servants, a tall, burly fellow named Israel. Have you seen him?"

"Sometimes he hangs about one of my kitchen maids, but not tonight, sir."

The newcomer turned and looked in Joseph's direction with some surprise. He made his way over to him, and the rough crowd of men separated respectfully to let him pass.

"I am Ralph Isaacs. You appear to be a stranger here, and, if you will forgive me for saying so, this is no lodging place for a gentleman. Allow me to guide you elsewhere." As they drove along in Isaacs's carriage, the two young men found they had many interests in common. Joseph was impressed with Isaacs's sophistication and his knowledge of Charleston. As they parted, he thanked his new-found friend for quite possibly saving his life.

Within a few days the young doctor found a permanent room in the home of two sisters who were friends of General Nathaniel Green, a business associate of his father. His medical practice grew, and his ability as a poet, combined with considerable personal charm, made him quite popular in Charleston society. Possessed of a normally happy disposition, the twenty-two-year-old doctor often whistled an English ballad as he bounded up the stairs. The two ladies began to look forward to the sound of that cheerful whistle that accompanied the comings and goings of their personable lodger.

Joseph and Ralph Isaacs continued to be very friendly, often attending parties and the theater together. But Isaacs, although brilliant and clever, was moody at times and unfortunately given to jealousy. As his young doctor friend's social prominence grew, he began to resent the popularity that came to Joseph so easily. At times his comments were cutting, if not actually hostile.

One evening they both attended the Shakespearean drama *Richard III*, but they were not seated together. Joseph's seat was somewhat better, for one's place in the Dock Theater was based on social standing. Isaacs, a proud man, must have resented this bitterly. The actress, a Miss Barrett, spoke her lines so softly that she could scarcely be heard and was so inexperienced as to be hopelessly inadequate. Joseph, however, was much taken with her.

Riding home in Isaacs's carriage, the two men argued about the quality of the play. What began as a difference of opinion became a violent quarrel, with Isaacs undoubtedly transferring some of his anger over his inferior seat in the theater to the matter they were discussing. He became bitterly sarcastic about Joseph's taste or lack of it. The two men must have related their opinions to others and aired their argument in public. Isaacs would not let it drop and took every opportunity to blacken the doctor's name.

Young Brown very foolishly retaliated by writing a letter to the Charleston *Gazette*, saying, "I account it one of the misfortunes of my life that I became intimate with that man." His words were to prove prophetic.

Isaacs wrote a vicious reply, accusing Doctor Brown of being a "self-created doctor and as blasted a scoundrel as ever disgraced humanity." All his envy and humiliation over watching the young man shine more brightly in society than himself found an outlet in this attempt to ruin his former friend.

Joseph Ladd Brown, in the heat of anger over Isaacs's reply, took the advice of some hot-headed friends and challenged Isaacs to a duel. Isaacs accepted, and the time was set for the next morning. (Dueling to settle matters of honor was a common practice in South Carolina and persisted into the late 1800s.) It was said later that Doctor Brown regretted his hasty challenge almost as soon as he had made it.

Early the next morning the two men, escorted by seconds and friends, met in a field near the edge of the city. Care was taken so that neither would have the disadvantage of the bright morning sun. They stood back to back, then walked off twenty paces and turned to face each other.

Brown had already decided what he would do. He raised his pistol high and fired toward the sky. Then he lowered the gun to his side and stood motionless. Isaacs gave him a long look and then deliberately raised his pistol and fired twice, each time hitting Brown in the legs below the knees. His intent was to cripple the doctor for life. Brown fell to the ground, blood spurting from the wounds. As a horrified crowd gathered around the young doctor, Isaacs, head held high and eyes blazing with fury, walked alone to his carriage.

Joseph was carried back to the home of the sisters, where he had first roomed, and for three weeks he lingered between life and death. A physician friend removed the bullets and attempted to make him more comfortable, but infection set in and no remedies of the day were effective. After considerable suffering, the young man died.

Afterwards, the sisters and others living in the house told a surprising story. Sometimes, when the late afternoon dusk cast shadows on the cobblestones, they heard the sound of footsteps bounding up the stairs. Then, as they listened in amazement, they heard the strains of a merry English ballad—a young man whistling a haunting melody. And so the story goes, lingering through the centuries.

Many lives have been lived out in this house. Additions have been made, such as the upstairs screened porch and the piazza below with its jogging board, one of those delights that a little girl may have played upon. It is a rare house indeed that never shelters children, and in this respect the House on Church Street follows convention. Among those who lived here were the children of the Savage family, who occupied it into the 1830s.

In 1941 the present owners bought this romantic, historic home. The mistress of the house tells an interesting present-day story about it. "A few years ago a well-known psychic came here. She asked if she might go upstairs alone, and I told her. 'Of course.' When she came back down she said, 'I felt the presence of the doctor, but even more strongly, I felt the presence of a little girl in the drawing room. Who was she?' I had no idea. But the strangest thing occurred last year when we were repairing the slate roof and had a section removed. Beneath it was a large squirrel's nest, and one of the workmen brought me something he had found under it.

"It was the dress of a little girl, and it must have been 150 years old. The tiny buttons were hand-carved bone."

What was the name of that little girl, and why should her presence still be felt on the second floor of this old house that seems to have more than one spirit? A tall, regal woman, this owner is also intrigued by the mystery. Originally an Ohioan, she came to Charleston forty years ago and has lived in the house ever since.

I wrote this on the day after Thanksgiving in Charleston. The temperature was in the seventies, and golden butterflies fluttered across the formal garden within the high walls. The gates were closed to protect the privacy of the owner and, perhaps, other secrets of a house that shelters the spirits of young Doctor Joseph Ladd Brown and a little girl—a little girl who once bounced up and down joyfully on the piazza jogging board and wore a dress with hand-carved whalebone buttons.

———————————

This house on Church Street was built about 1732. Here a 22-year-old man died more than 200 years ago. His ghost has been said to haunt the lovely old home. It is a private residence and not available for tours.

HOTEL DEL CORONADO

Coronado, California

On a balmy beach by the blue Pacific, across from San Diego, is an elegant hotel that has become a legend, the Hotel del Coronado. Just a visit to this old hotel is a unique experience, as countless others have found. The Prince of Wales (Edward VIII), Ronald Reagan, Richard Nixon, Lyndon B. Johnson, Marilyn Monroe, John Wayne, Shirley MacLaine, and numerous other celebrities have all enjoyed its 1880s mystique.

Built when President Grover Cleveland was in the White House and Wyatt Earp was keeping order in Tombstone, the Hotel del Coronado is a National Historic Landmark. One of the last great seaside resorts, the hotel offers, along with its palatial interior and excellent food, a magnificent expanse of ocean. It also offers a haunted room.

As I drove down Orange Avenue in Coronado, I scanned each side of the avenue carefully, hoping to see the hotel; yet I was totally unprepared for my first view of it. When I first saw the cluster of buildings, it was like nothing I had ever seen out west. Something about it reminded me of a huge colony of many different-sized mushrooms huddled together, each capped with a pointed red Mediterranean roof—a sort of Cape May, New Jersey, compressed through a telephoto lens.

We parked the car and went in through a back entrance, which was not imposing, unless you wanted to count seeing the suite of rooms that was reserved for the Reagans' stays here when Mr. Reagan was governor of California. This entrance opens upon an immense courtyard surrounded by the hotel.

A few feet away from me stood a bridal couple under the white Victorian gazebo, exchanging their vows. I will confess that, as the minister intoned away, I was somewhat startled, for I had almost walked out on the green and joined the attendants. Some people enjoy watching weddings, but, since I find researching ghosts more entertaining, I went to the main lobby.

133

The legendary Hotel del Coronado near San Diego has a room said to be haunted.

As I made my way toward the desk, it was necessary to move quickly to avoid colliding with a lady holding a tape player in her hand and staring upward at the most enormous crystal chandelier I have ever seen. She gazed at it entranced, swaying back and forth squarely in front of me with eyes like those of a bird under the spell of a snake. I learned later that she was taking the guided tour of this historic hotel and had probably just heard the narrator on the tape say that it took a crew of six men six months to take the chandelier down and clean it.

At the desk the assistant manager replied to my question about a haunted room by saying abruptly, "We do not have a haunted room." I nodded politely and asked to see the manager. The manager said, "We do have a room that some people say is haunted, but I don't think it is."

"Would it be possible for me to see the room?"

"No, I'm sorry but it wouldn't."

That seemed an astounding reply, and I went on to explain that I was writing a book on stories of this sort from all over the United States. Again, I asked to view the room. Again, he refused.

"Would you like to rent it?" he asked

"What number is it?"

"Number 3502."

How odd that he would know the number of the room if it were not haunted. Certainly, something must have happened in this particular room, I thought. "Well, what is the price?"

"It would be one hundred and five dollars."

"Could you show me the room?"

"I can't show you the room. I'm sorry, ma'am." Again, his refusal to allow me to see the room was surprising. Was there really something in the room? And if there was, it would scarcely make itself known in the middle of the day.

"Thank you. We will let you know later," I said, having thought of another approach, but one that could wait until after lunch.

It was Sunday, and there was a sumptuous buffet in the majestic Crown Room. A lavish display of delicacies was spread upon the long tables, and it was possible, through a door I had passed earlier, to glimpse at least a dozen different varieties of luscious-looking desserts. As we lunched, I thought of the famous people who had dined here in this room with its magnificent, vaulted oak ceiling. I was sitting in the very room where Charles Lindbergh had been honored at a banquet after his solo flight across the Atlantic in 1927. The Prince of Wales had been feted here as well, and, unfortunately for a now-forgotten gentleman named Simpson, his wife, Wallis, was a guest on that occasion. . . .

After a delightful brunch, I felt eager to return to the main lobby and resume my ghost-story quest. Just around the corner from the main desk was another desk where guests were engaging bellboys, and I decided to ask one of the young men whether he knew of any stories about Room 3502.

"I don't know anything about it, but if anyone does, it will be Steve Oakford. He knows all about this hotel. He is over at the other building now, but I'm sure he will be back in a few minutes."

From then on, to every bellboy that came up I said, "Steve?" until I finally found the right one. When I began to ask him questions, I wondered whether he really was the right one.

"I'm sorry, but I never discuss anything personal about our guests," he said in answer to my first question about the room. Of course, the guest in question could scarcely be very sensitive to gossip, having been dead for many years.

"Steve, I wouldn't dream of asking you to repeat anything about anyone, nor am I doing so now."

"That's why I have been here so long. Our guests value the privacy they have."

"I'm sorry, I don't believe I am making myself clear. My only interest is in what sort of story is told about Room 3502. I have heard there is a ghost story connected with it."

"Madam, I am a born again Christian."

"So am I, but it has never interfered with my interest in folklore or how stories of this sort begin."

"Someone who once worked here started the story, and I have never believed it."

There was no more to be learned from Steve, but from talk around the hotel, I discovered that most employees had heard that the room was haunted, and some believed it.

Kate Morgan was born in Dubuque, Iowa, three years after the close of the Civil War. Her father was a well-to-do farmer, and, when she was a child, her parents gave the lovely, golden-haired little Kate every advantage. She was in her early teens when her mother died. Her father remarried, and, despite Kate's efforts to please her stepmother, Maggie, she was never able to do so. As time went on, her life became more and more miserable.

The lovely clothes her father had once bought her were now tattered and outgrown. Anything Morgan did for his daughter made her stepmother extremely jealous. Her father's just bringing her a bright ribbon from the store was an occasion for harsh words. Even in her worn dresses, however, Kate's beauty shone through as bright as a ray of sunshine.

In 1868 Dubuque, Iowa, on a small scale, showed all the promise and all the tawdry glitter of the city it would one day become. The bootclad feet of rough cattlemen with plenty of money to spend trod the muddy streets, and there were gambling houses that promised more money still. There were demure, well-dressed ladies carrying parasols to shield their delicate complexions from the rays of the strong, Midwest sun. And then there were those whose hair boasted a brassy brilliance, whose lips and cheeks were as red as the blossoms of the trumpet vines that twined over a porch rail. The good women could spot them in a twinkling, and Maggie Morgan's sharp tongue was ever ready to point them out.

While Maggie lay in bed, resting, Kate was often sent from her father's farm through the countryside, bright with purple phlox and wild roses, into town to purchase fresh vegetables and other supplies. One July afternoon, she had just come out of the Dubuque Supply Company, carrying her purchases, when one of the cattlemen spoke to her.

"You sure are a pretty gal. Let's go have a drink," Bill Bailey said.

Kate shook her head and started to pass him. When she was level with him on the wooden sidewalk, one big, calloused hand reached out, grabbed her by the elbow, and spun her around to face him.

"I don't know you, sir. Please, let go my arm."

"Wal, you can git to know me mighty fast!" With that, he jerked Kate toward him, and her bag full of groceries fell from her arms, its contents spilling all over the ground.

"I seen you before, wearin' them raggedy clothes. You need a purty dress, a gal like you." He encircled her waist with his arm, thrusting his bearded face close to Kate's own. When he did, she screamed and tried to pull away. A knot of men began to gather around them. Kate strained to get away from the man with all her strength, and, as she did, her dress tore at the shoulder. She began crying.

"Now, see what you went and done," Bill said, leering at her. "I tole you, you need a purty dress, and, after we get it, I'll take you home."

"You're not taking her anywhere," said a man's voice from the crowd. Bill Bailey looked up in surprise at the man, as the little audience parted respectfully for him to pass. He was a tall, well-built fellow with bright blue eyes and dark-brown curly hair, and his expensive clothes showed that he was not one of the other cattlemen.

Bailey released Kate and started for the stranger. He stopped abruptly when the man's hand slid toward his pocket, for he knew what that meant. If the pocket concealed a small pistol, Bailey didn't want a confrontation. He turned away and melted into the little knot of onlookers. The stranger threw his own jacket around Kate's shoulders and began picking up the contents of her bag while she thanked him.

"I just want to see that you get safely home," he replied. "What is your name?"

"Kate Morgan. And yours, sir?"

"Lou Garrou."

She rode behind him on his horse, and the horse picked its way slowly along, Garrou obviously in no hurry. He had gotten off a Mississippi riverboat that afternoon and was in town to enjoy himself for a few days. In answer to a question about his occupation, he replied that he was a "businessman" and that his business required constant travel. In a day or two he would be moving on. He came back to see Kate that night and appeared at the door of the farmhouse the following afternoon with a box of pretty clothes for her. When he was still there at suppertime, the hospitable Morgan invited him to sit down and share their meal.

When Garrou showed up about noon on the third day, he asked Morgan if he could marry Kate. The surprised farmer told Garrou that he didn't think they knew enough about him. Lou began talking about leaving the business he was in because it required too much travel and settling down with Kate on some land of their own. Kate's father liked the sound of that, and her stepmother, eager to get rid of the girl, sided with Lou.

A justice of the peace married them. After the ceremony, her father pressed a fifty-dollar note in her hand. It was the first time since her mother's death that Kate had seen her father with tears in his eyes. As the late afternoon sun turned the river to gold, the pair boarded one of the packets heading south on the Mississippi to Savannah, Fulton, Comanche, and Moline. The very names of all these unknown, glamorous places were exciting to Kate. When the big paddles were rhythmically pounding the water and the riverboat was well underway, Kate found out what Lou's "business" was. He was a gambler.

That night she cried and told him he had deceived her. He became angry and asked her what difference did his business make if she cared about him, and, if she didn't, she could always go home. But Kate knew her stepmother would not welcome her back. There was nothing for her to do but make the best of it.

From then on the girl traveled everywhere with her husband. When it was not on riverboats, it was to cities like San Francisco or San Diego, anywhere Lou could find games with high enough stakes. Usually, she registered under the name Mrs. Anderson Barnard. Whether this was Lou's real name or one he had chosen to protect his identity, Kate never knew. But she did know that sometimes after the card games there were angry losers.

After a few years she settled in Visalia, California, while he went on from place to place. Sometimes he would show up unexpectedly, promise to change, stay for a week or so, and then leave again. During one of these visits, Kate asked him if they couldn't live like other people did. He told her they would buy a little house in Los Angeles and start a family.

They bought the house there, as he had promised, and for a while Lou seemed happy. Because he was happy, so was Kate. There were plenty of games around town, and enough money rolled in. It seemed too good to be true. Lou tried hard to be careful and not get too greedy. He would win a few games, then lose one or two, keeping his bets small. But after four or five months, he began to get restless and complain. It was just as it had always been when they stayed anywhere for longer than a few months. The stakes in the games around town weren't big enough, or there was more money to be made in San Francisco or Sacramento. And then one night, he just didn't come home. He had never done that before. It was October of 1892, and not long afterward Kate found that she was pregnant.

One afternoon just before Thanksgiving, a letter arrived from Lou. He wrote that he didn't think he would ever be able to settle down, and it wasn't right for a pretty woman like her to be tied to a drifter like himself. He would see her in a few weeks and give her money for a divorce. She could keep the house. He had no use for one.

Kate was heartbroken, but she knew that when he found out about the baby, he would change his mind. One of his favorite haunts was the Hotel del Coronado in San Diego. There was money she had saved for an emergency under the elaborate black-and-gold French clock he had once given her, and the next day she bought some lovely clothes with part of it. She would go to San Diego and talk with him. He would be happy over her news, and perhaps they could live there. Everything would be the way it was during the early years, except now there would be the three of them.

When she arrived at the Hotel del Coronado, she registered as Mrs. Lottie Anderson Barnard and said she was awaiting her brother's arrival. That afternoon Kate went through the hotel to the game room. When she looked in the door, there sat Lou, playing cards at a table, and behind him was a woman with her arms looped familiarly around his neck as if he belonged to her. You might have heard a heart break, you might have heard a tear drop, if either were possible. Lou did not look up. Kate never entered the room. Turning away, she walked through the vast lobby out to one of the carriages sitting in front of the hotel and gave the driver the address of a shop in San Diego. Two hours later, when the carriage deposited her once more in front of the hotel, her handbag was heavy with the weight of a .44-caliber pistol. It had begun to rain.

Back in room 302, Kate unfolded the pretty clothes she had bought the day before she left Los Angeles, threw them in the fire-place, and touched the newspaper beneath the kindling with one of the large wooden matches from the small white china box on the mantel. Then she took from her suitcase a picture set in a medallion on a woven-hair bracelet, looked at it, and threw it into the fire. Last to go into the flames was her pocketbook. Putting on her coat, Kate picked up a paper bag containing the gun and started down the long, carpeted hallway to the elevator. The ornate brass elevator cage closed behind her. Was there anything else she should do? Yes, one more thing. "Is Mr. Lou Garrou registered here?" she asked, stopping at the desk.

The clerk went through the cards on the rack. "Yes, madam. Through Sunday, I believe."

"May I have a piece of paper?" The attractive, blonde-haired young woman wrote three sentences on it. *Lottie Barnard was registered in room 302. She loved you very much. She came to tell you your child was on the way.* "Can you have someone take this to him in the game room in about fifteen minutes?"

"Of course, madam."

When Kate went out the hotel door leading to the oceanfront veranda, the rain had become a fierce storm. There was the angry rumble of thunder, and crashing bolts of lightning split the sky asunder, illuminating the veranda. The young woman reached into the paper bag, placed the pistol barrel to her right temple, and fired once. Muffled by the crashing dissonance of the storm, the shot went unheard. But by early morning her water-soaked body had been found, and a crowd of shocked guests were gathered on the veranda. Whether a gambler who called himself Lou Garrou was among them, no one will ever know.

Opinions of the hotel staff vary from denial of anything happening at all to abject fear of whatever occurs in the room that was once Room 302 and is now 3502. An examination of the floor plan of the hotel in 1892 reveals a larger room with a fireplace and without the present built-in bathroom, but the room number does correspond to the room rented by Mrs. Lottie Anderson Barnard.

One of the elevator operators was more communicative than some of the other staff. He told of guests who had questioned him about eerie lights flickering outside 3502 and one who had seen a lady in an old-fashioned dress and coat, soaked to the bone, standing in front of the door to the room late at night. He mentioned maids hearing the sound of weeping on stormy nights when they passed the room, only to discover, when they unlocked the door to clean the following morning, that the room had been unoccupied the night before. Several of the maids seemed actually fearful, as if the young woman, just as she was found that Wednesday morning of 1892 lying dead on the veranda in her sodden dress and coat, might sometimes at night drift back down the long corridor until she reached her former room.

Over the years the story has been told that various articles are disturbed in the room and that highly unusual things take place there because it is inhabited by the anguished spirit of this unfortunate young woman. It would appear that poor Kate's greatest mistake was to leave one set of unhappy circumstances for another far more tragic. If it is stormy some night at the Hotel del Coronado, will a guest meet a lovely woman near room 3502 in an 1890s dress dripping with water? Does she still return to grieve over her gambler husband and her unborn child?

Kate, Kate, you chose a gambler for a mate. Kate, Kate, was he worth your baby's fate?

There is no resort hotel on either coast that can quite match the del Coronado, and certainly none with a more interesting guest list of the famous who have stayed there. Whether you rent room 3502 or not, it will be an experience. For reservations or information, write to the Hotel del Coronado, 1500 Orange Avenue, Coronado, California 92118 or telephone (619) 435-6611.

THE HERMITAGE

Murrell's Inlet, South Carolina

There are few people alive or dead more famous locally than lovely young Alice Flagg, who once lived at the Hermitage in Murrell's Inlet, South Carolina. This fact is most amazing, as it was more than a century ago that the sixteen-year-old Alice went to school in Charleston, studied, danced, fell passionately in love, and died a tragic death. Generations of young people have visited her grave under the moss-draped oaks at All Saints Waccamaw Church. Reports continue to this day that the ghost of Alice still haunts her old home and roams the marshes of Murrell's Inlet.

Dr. Allard Belin Flagg built the house in 1848, choosing a point of land surrounded on three sides by tidal marshes. He placed it within a grove of live oaks that at that time were at least one hundred years old, and they are still there. Today, a winding dirt road bordered with cedars leads off Highway 17 to the Hermitage. Although it was never a *Gone with the Wind* antebellum home, the first view of the Hermitage is that of a house with character and serenity in a setting of a green lawn and huge trees. Across the front porch are immense white columns, each carved from a single tree.

Reilly Burns, a serious young engineer who visited the house from out of state, tells his own experience.

"Often after my arrival in Myrtle Beach, the story would come up, and each time I would make some skeptical or sarcastic comment. Finally I decided to investigate for myself and see if there really was an apparition of a girl named Alice.

"When I arrived at the Hermitage, the Willcoxes welcomed me as cordially as if I had been an invited guest rather than someone who had arrived unannounced. Clarke Willcox and his wife, Lillian, were warmly hospitable and seemed to enjoy showing me around the house. The flooring was of beautiful twenty-foot lengths of heart pine, and dowel trim expertly done by slaves decorates the front parlor. Upstairs

The Hermitage at Murrell's Inlet near Myrtle Beach is haunted by one of the state's most famous ghosts. (Photo by Bruce Roberts.)

over the front porch is an unusual round-hinged window with curved spokes and a central eye.

"'She probably looked out that window many a time, for that was Alice's bedroom,' said Clarke Willcox, gesturing toward the room on my right as I stood with my back to the round window. The room was white, as was the spread on the spool bed. Over a door hung a needlework sampler upon which had been worked, in large letters, the name 'Alice.' It was a room that might have been typical of any young girl before the Civil War, what with its dainty, ruffled curtains, its innocence, its simplicity. I glanced in perfunctorily but made no comment.

"When we sat down on the porch, we continued to talk about the house. The front steps and walk are of sturdy English ballast brick, used to prevent light sailboats from capsizing in midocean. When not needed, these bricks were often thrown into harbors and rivers, and many of them, when retrieved, paved the streets of Charleston and Savannah. It appeared that Willcox was not going to bring up the subject of Alice, which I had been prepared to ask questions about, questions that, in the light of my host's obvious intelligence and culture, now seemed somewhat rude.

"'Everyone who comes here probably asks you to tell them the story about Alice,' I finally said, leading into the subject in a manner that I felt did not indicate either belief or unbelief.

"'You are right,' my host replied, 'and with so many questions about the story, I suppose that I have thought about her almost daily during the years we have lived in the house. No description of the Hermitage would really be complete without the tragedy of Alice Flagg. I gather you wish to hear it?' I nodded, and Willcox began his story.

"'Alice was the sixteen-year-old sister of Dr. Allard Belin Flagg, who built the Hermitage. Since there was a considerable age difference between Allard and his young sister, and since their father was dead, Allard always dominated his sister. He was more like a parent than a brother, and at times a tyrannical and disapproving parent at that.

"'On her last vacation at home from finishing school in Charleston, Alice wore her new engagement ring on a ribbon around her neck beneath her blouse, unable to brave Allard's rage if he saw it. She did everything possible even to conceal her happiness, for she was aware of his contempt for a man who was in the turpentine industry, a mere merchant, rather than of the professional or planter class.

"'She returned to school after Christmas, and that spring was one of joy and secret planning for the future with her fiancé. The high point of the social season each year was the Spring Ball, at which the debutantes were presented. Alice made her debut in the most beautiful white gown imaginable. Those who saw her commented on how lovely she looked and on the becoming color in her cheeks as she danced one dance after another with her fiancé. Her mother was not able to attend for she had fled from the Low Country, with its dread malaria season, off to the mountains. Fortunately, young Allard was not present either, but visiting patients and operating the farm.

"'The day following the ball, Alice was suddenly stricken with the fever prevalent in the area. School authorities sent for Dr. Flagg. After equipping the family carriage with medications and articles for Alice's comfort, he set out with a servant over the miserable roads to Charleston. It was a four-day trip one way from Murrell's Inlet, and there were five rivers to ford.

"'When they arrived back at the Hermitage, he was able to give his young sister a more thorough examination, and, in doing so, he found the ring. Allard snatched it from her neck with such force that the ribbon broke. Then he strode outdoors and threw the ring in the creek. Alice was brokenhearted, and, when visitors would come to her sickroom, she would beg them to find her ring. Her distress was apparent to all, and finally a young cousin went to Georgetown and bought a ring. When he pressed it into her hand, weak and near death as she was, she knew the difference. She threw it on the floor and begged him to find *her* ring.

"'The last of the week following her arrival at home, Alice breathed her last. There was not sufficient time for her mother even to get back from the mountains before the casket was closed, and Alice was buried temporarily here in the yard of the Hermitage. When her mother returned, the girl's body was moved to the family plot at All Saints Waccamaw Church, on the river opposite Pawley's Island. Beneath the beautiful trees in the old cemetery and amidst the imposing stones raised in memory of the other Flaggs may be seen a flat, white-marble slab. Upon it is engraved the single word *Alice*.

"'It is a telling sort of epitaph in its simplicity. I would say it would be given only to one who was unknown save for her first name, or so beloved that only the first name was needed. I have walked through that cemetery many a time and seen a vase of flowers on her grave, a tribute to her left by some unknown donor. People are very romantic, aren't they?'

"'Do you think Alice really does come back?' I asked Mr. Willcox.

"'People have been seeing the ghost of Alice Flagg for a hundred years or more. They were seeing it when I was a boy.'

"'When she appears, what does she do?'

"'Old people in the area say that she is searching for her ring and that her spirit won't rest until she finds it.'

"'Does she ever come back here to the house?'

"'My wife and I have often felt her presence in her bedroom. An aunt of mine slept in that room while I was growing up. One day, when she was looking in the mirror and brushing her hair, she suddenly saw a lovely girl in a white dress reflected in the mirror beside her. She turned, and no one was there. Aunt Emma screamed all the way down the stairs,' he said, chuckling.

"'Then there are some who claim to have conjured up her ghost in the cemetery.' Willcox stared thoughtfully out over the salt marshes. 'Some nights I think she is out there or even under the trees on the lawn, searching for the ring, never giving up her quest. I've looked for it myself, but if I ever found it, I wouldn't know what to do with it. How could I get it back to her?'

"'Where is Alice's grave located in the cemetery?'

"'Beyond the church on the right. You're going out there, aren't you?'

"'I probably will.' The sun had set by now, and it was getting chilly on the porch. We both stood up, and I thanked him gratefully for his kindness.

"It was time for dinner, and I looked forward to eating at Oliver's or one of the other seafood restaurants on Highway 17. I thought it would be best for me to go out to the cemetery in the morning. The meal was delicious, but, as I ate, I was more and more tempted to find Alice's grave that night. If the moon was out, it might be possible; if not, there was no hope at all in the darkness.

"The sky was clouded over and there was no sign of the moon or even a star. I drove south on Highway 17, and somehow, without even being able to help it, my car turned right and took the road to All Saints Waccamaw Cemetery. At least I had a powerful flashlight in the trunk that I could shine on some of the stones, but trying to find her slab that night was risky.

"By the time I pulled up and stopped beside the old cemetery, I was beginning to feel foolish. If anyone passed and saw my light bobbing about out there, would they think I was a vandal or perhaps even a grave robber? There were the gates of the cemetery. Would they be locked? They opened easily, and, as I went in, I closed and latched them carefully behind me. Where had Willcox said her grave was? Somewhere beyond the church . . . past the front steps and then to the right? Was that where he had meant?

"I shone my light on one of the stones, but it was not a member of the Flagg family. Off in the distance a dog howled mournfully. Wasn't that considered an omen of death? I didn't know whether I was nervous or just felt foolish being here on such a mission. Sometimes I bumped into markers, and that gave me a real start. At other times I would step on a sunken grave and feel my feet sink down still further into the soft, sandy soil.

"For more than thirty minutes I must have wandered about the cemetery with no success. It was not easy to find a flat stone at night. And then I stepped on it. When I did, I jumped to one side, for the act of standing on someone's gravestone seemed sacrilegious. I shone the light down squarely on the white marble, and there, engraved in large letters, was the name "Alice." My excitement was so great that I dropped the light, and, as it hit the stone, it went out. It didn't really matter, though, because I had found her grave. With my index finger I traced the letters. It was the stone I had been looking for!

"Someone had said that teenagers often come out here at night and walk around the grave thirteen times, hoping to commune with Alice's spirit. At least there was none of that foolishness going on tonight, for I seemed to be the only one in the cemetery. I had taken a picture of the Hermitage and wanted to take a picture of the stone, just as a curiosity, of course. But I could come back here in the morning before I left and do that. It was getting quite misty, and even a flash shot might not turn out well.

"'What are you doing down there on the ground?' asked a feminine voice.

I turned around. Behind me stood a girl who must have come up without my hearing her. It was probably one of the teenagers who often visited the gravesite. "'I was looking for the grave of a girl named Alice.'

"'You have found it,' she replied.

"'Do you come here often?'

"'Oh, I'm out here quite a lot, most often when some of my friends are visiting.'

"'Isn't it pretty foolish for you and your friends to come out here in this old cemetery to see the grave of a girl who has been dead more than one hundred years?'

"'You make that sound like a very long time.'

"'Isn't it?'

"'Why, it doesn't seem long to me at all.' As she talked I thought her dress appeared almost luminous. The moonlight must have been shining on it. I looked up at the sky, and the moon was out for the first time that night.

"'Why did you come out here?' asked the girl.

"'I suppose I wanted to know if all the stories I had heard were true and if there really was such a thing as the spirit of a beautiful girl named Alice.'

"'What a ridiculous question.' My heart began to hammer.

"'Do you mean you are Alice?' Her white raiment was glowing ever brighter until I could scarcely look at it.

"'Of course I am Alice, and my home is over at the Hermitage.'

"'Then what are you doing here in this cemetery?' I asked more boldly, but she ignored my question.

"'Did you come to help me?'

"'That depends. What would you like for me to do?'

"'I want you to help me find my ring. I've been looking for it ever so long.'

"'I'm not sure I can do that. Your brother threw it away, you know.'

"'How could he do something so wicked? Where could it be?'

"'I am sorry, but no one really knows but your brother.'

"While she talked her dress became so bright that I had to turn my eyes away. A cloud of mist came rolling up from the river and enveloped us. As we entered the cloud, for the first time I was afraid.

"'If I ever see Allard Flagg, I will surely tell him . . . ,' she was saying, and her voice faded. When the cloud finally passed, the girl was gone, and so was the moon. I heard the angry rumble of thunder in the distance, the prelude to a coming storm. For the first time in my life I found myself trembling violently. My eyes had been exposed to such brilliant light that they were not readjusting well, and the darkness of the cemetery was overwhelming.

"What in the name of heaven and earth had happened to the practical, down-to-earth engineer whom I had always considered myself to be? Without my flashlight, how would I find the gate? Suddenly, I heard a metallic clang, and I realized that someone had closed the gate noisily. Was I imagining that I heard the rattle of a chain securing it? Had a night watchman locked me in?

"In my haste to get out, I stumbled over a footstone and barely managed to keep from falling. I stretched my arm out in front of me for some protection, and my fingers rested on a cold marble face. Whether the face was that of an angel or Christ, I was not sure, for I didn't leave my hand there long enough to find out. Finally, I managed to make my way to the gate. Automatically, I reached for the latch to open it, and when I did, I discovered that I could have walked right through it. Instead of being closed, the gate was standing ajar. What about the sound I had just heard? Hadn't I been careful to latch it behind me? Yes, I was certain I had."

Gate or not, Reilly Burns has become a believer, I thought as I drove down Highway 17 north toward Myrtle Beach. That night I lay on the bed in my motel room with my hands clasped behind my head, and stared at the ceiling for a long, long time.

———————————

The Hermitage is just south of Myrtle Beach on Highway 17 at Murrell's Inlet. Clarke Willcox is always most cordial to visitors. Telephone (803) 357-1205.

CARNTON HOUSE

Franklin, Tennessee

Up the curving drive, set far back from the road, Carnton House stands alone in a grove of maple trees, its darkened windows staring out from between tall, white columns. Paul Levitt thought that there was something lonely and mysterious about it.

November 30th had been a golden autumn day, but only a little daylight was left, for it was late afternoon with darkness falling fast. As Paul drove up to the house, he realized he had arrived too late. It was just after five, and tour guides would already have left. Well, it didn't matter. He would get out anyway and walk about the grounds. All was quiet. Only the faint crunching sounds of his footsteps could be heard on the gravel drive. He was in a mood to be alone, to think and to absorb the atmosphere of this place that his friend, John Carter, had described.

"There will never be another Carnton House," Carter had said. "Never a place that's seen such tragedy and grief."

Underfoot, a profusion of leaves lay like a golden treasure spread out by some profligate Midas. It seemed almost wrong to tread upon such beauty. Bending down, Paul picked up one perfect, five-pointed yellow maple leaf, then another; but on the second leaf were splotches of crimson, bright as blood.

It reminded him of how many men had bled and died here. What was it his great-grandmother in Ohio once said? Something like "Your great-grandaddy was in a terrible battle at a place called Franklin." He was walking over the same ground where his ancestor had fought. Wasn't it a strange coincidence that today was the anniversary of that struggle? It lasted just five hours, but what a bloody, disastrous battle it had been.

He walked without considering the time, for he was in no hurry to return to the motel. He found the pressures of his work beginning to leave him and felt strangely relaxed as, almost automatically, his feet

Carnton House is probably Tennessee's most well-known haunted house, where spirits have been authenticated by too many to shrug away. (Photo by Bruce Roberts.)

followed a path that led from the house across the fields. Where was he going? Did it matter?

Finally, the path brought him around to the back of the house, and near the porch he saw the silhouette of a man who appeared to be getting on a horse. If the fellow paused, he would speak to him. On second thought, he would take the initiative and hail him. "Hello, there. I might be mistaken, but I thought I saw you about to get on a horse. What happened to him?"

"The same thing that happened to my own horse, shot from under me. But I suppose it doesn't matter. Whether you ride or whether you go on foot, you are still at their mercy tonight."

This was strange talk. Paul wasn't frightened, but he did find himself tingling slightly. By now both men were standing on the porch.

"If you're coming with me, you had better find a pistol or a carbine; otherwise you won't last long out there. But not many of us are going to live through tonight, anyway."

What was he talking about? thought Paul, now close enough to see the man fairly well. He had a mustache, a short beard, and eyes that bored straight through you, and he stood there in the after dusk, humming to himself.

"We are a band of brothers and native to the soil, hm, hm, hm, hmm. . . . And when our rights were threatened, the cry rose near and far, hurray, for the Bonnie Blue Flag that bears a single star."

Good lord, thought Paul, they must be having one of those battle reenactments out there today, and this fellow thinks that I am part of it. From his dress Paul assumed the man was an officer. His hat was black cloth with small gilt buttons on the sides and strands of gold braid that met in the front in a four-leaf clover without a stem. He wore it with the leather visor pulled down, almost as if he were trying to protect his face. At his belt were not only a carbine and pistol, but a long sword as well.

"What kind of carbine is that you're wearing?"

"It's an Enfield .577. What do you have?"

"Me? Nothing. Man, I've just seen them in books. I never shot one, or a pistol, either. And a sword, I wouldn't know what to do with that."

Even in the poor light, the stranger looked astonished. "You had better go over to the Carter house or into town then, for this is no place for you tonight. That fool Hood thinks he's as brilliant as Lee, but he's sending my men to be slaughtered!" The officer's voice rose in anger. Then he seemed to be talking to someone by his side. "They have three lines of works, and they are all completed."

If there was a reply, Paul didn't hear it. But he did hear the officer call out once more, and, above the rustle of autumn leaves, the words floated back to him strong and clear. "Well, Govan, if we are to die, let us die like men!"

With that, Paul saw the stranger, who had never bothered to introduce himself, fling his cap into the air in a violent, angry gesture and then disappear. From the distance came the command, "Charge men! Charge! Do you hear me, do you hear . . . " And the sound of the voice faded away in a hailstorm of shot and shell, musketry and cannons.

Then smoke, or was it mist, seemed to lie all about him. He thought he heard the music of a regiment band, and the song was "Annie Laurie."

A few seconds later came the most frightening sound Paul had ever heard. A veritable chorus of men's voices shattered the air with the fierce, bloodcurdling cry that Union Troops called the Rebel Yell.

Paul Levitt did what many raw recruits had done when they heard that yell. He began to run. As he ran, his heart pounded. He seemed to be surrounded by the din of thousands of small arms firing and the roar of shells. The very atmosphere was pervaded with death. He thought he was heading back to his car, but, losing his sense of direction, he found himself stumbling about in the graveyard not far from the house. It was a cemetery provided by Carnton shortly after the battle, for a day later more than 1,700 Confederate men lay dead in the fields near this home.

Finally Paul recovered himself and made his way back to his car. What was it his friend Carter had said? That "on this ground the dead once stood six men deep, so close they could not fall." Paul slept poorly, for all night long he dreamed that he was in the midst of one furious charge after another. But early the next morning he was out at the house again. If he had been part of some supernatural experience or seen a ghost, as he believed he had, he wanted to seek out clues that might help him understand. He was fortunate to arrive on a day when Bernice Seiberling was there. Mrs. Seiberling is a delightful, gray-haired lady who has a thorough knowledge of the history of Carnton and has been guiding visitors through the house for about seven years.

"I would imagine a house with this much history has some ghost stories connected with it," Paul said tentatively as a way to introduce the subject.

"Oh my, yes," said Mrs. Seiberling, not reluctant to share stories of some of the spirits heard from more frequently. And much to his surprise, she began to talk about a former cook at Carnton during Civil War days and the ghost's ways of getting attention.

"I had been aware of her for quite a while, for I would hear glasses clinking in the kitchen as if someone were washing dishes. Than I began to hear her in other areas of the house. One day I had a tour going, and it sounded as if rocks were being thrown at the windows and they were breaking.

"Most of the noises were coming from one room. When we reached it, we found a framed picture of the house lying face up on top of a heater, its glass shattered in a million pieces. It was as though someone had carefully placed it there. One of the men on the tour took his camera and made a picture of it, for he said 'it's impossible for that picture to have fallen in such a way.'

"On another occasion, I was here alone on a cold winter day and kept hearing something on a small enclosed porch off the back of the house, so I went to investigate. We keep a box of old glass panes on a shelf there. But what I found were two panes of unbroken glass, the thin old glass, one lying on each side of the door. The box, of course, was still on the shelf. It's as though the spirit has a sense of humor and likes to play tricks on me. We had all heard things but had no idea as to what was causing them until, one day, a descendant of the Carnton family said, 'You knew there had been a murder in this house, didn't you?'

"It seems that one of the field hands murdered a young girl in the kitchen in the early 1840s or before, probably due to some motive such as jealousy. There was real prejudice on the part of house servants toward those who did the heavy work on the plantation, and the girl may have rejected him or had another sweetheart.

"Sometimes it sounds exactly like dishes being washed. One night ten of us were all in the dining room having our regular board meeting of the Carnton Society. The lady sitting beside me turned to me and said, 'I think I hear someone in the kitchen.' I just said, 'No.' She turned to me again in a few minutes and said. 'I know someone is in there,' and this time I said, 'There is no one in the kitchen.' But she got up and went back there.

"When she returned and sat down, she had the strangest expression on her face. 'You are right,' she said, 'no one is there.' I told the other members of the board about hearing the cook and her antics, and they believed me. Even many visitors who come here ask me if we don't have spirits in the house. It amazes me that strangers seem to feel it, although, when there are lots of workmen around, we don't hear the spirits as much.

"One afternoon a workman saw a beautiful young girl with dark hair in the upstairs hall. He won't work up there now unless someone is with him. He was really upset. Whether it was one of the two surviving Carnton children who had grown into womanhood or not, I don't know. They lost three children out of five in infancy. That seems shocking to us, but many people didn't even live to middle age a hundred or so years ago."

Paul had begun to give up hope that he would hear any story that might relate to his own experience, when finally Mrs. Seiberling changed the subject.

"I hope you won't think I am silly when I tell you something else that has been reported to us here. Visitors say they have seen a Confederate soldier who walks the perimeter of this property. I don't laugh at them anymore, for there have been times in the late afternoon, especially in fall, when I have heard my own ghost soldier or, should I say, the sound of heavy footsteps. When I hear those striding feet, I hurry to look out, but the back veranda is always empty."

"This house was used as a hospital after the battle of Franklin, and the bodies of four Confederate generals were placed on that back porch. They were generals Grandberry, Adams, and Cleburne. But the general who was most loved was the Irishman Pat Cleburne, and all the next day men who had survived [the battle] filed past, paying their last respects to him. It is said that, when Cleburne died, the South lost a general second only to 'Stonewall' Jackson. Before he was buried, Mrs. McGavock took the general's cap and sword, later presenting them to the State of Tennessee Museum."

"What did the cap look like?" Paul asked.

"It was a round, black cap with little buttons on each side. I don't know how many. And there were strips of gold braid that came up to the front and ran into a four-leaf clover. Poor General Cleburne. They say he was a very brave man."

Black with gold braid, a four-leaf clover . . . . the words kept going through Levitt's mind, and, as Mrs. Seiberling went on talking, he missed part of what she was saying about the names of former residents of Carnton.

"People who have lived here and others in the area have reported hearing a Confederate soldier pace to and fro on the front porch. They come back and ask if I have heard him. I tell them, yes, I have heard him many times."

Struck by the similarity of the cap on the officer he had seen and the one belonging to the general, Levitt had heard what he had come to hear. He believed the stranger he had seen the evening before was none other than the spirit of General Pat Cleburne. How could he tell Mrs. Seiberling such a story? He simply let her talk on.

"I warn you, this house has a pull about it, and if you ever visit it, you'll come back," said Bernice Seiberling. "People return again and again."

"Return again and again" echoed in Paul's mind. And it may be that spirits do, too, he thought.

But most important of all, Carnton is a timeless place. It is a place where "the dead once stood . . . so close they could not fall," where bullets came thick as rain, and where soldiers pulled their caps down over their faces in a desperate, futile attempt to protect themselves. It is a place to shudder at men's ferocity toward other men. It is probably Tennessee's most haunted house, a house where spirits have been authenticated by too many to shrug away. If you sense this on your visit to Carnton, you will be among the many who have.

Carnton House is in Franklin, Tennessee, not far from Nashville. The house is open seven days a week except in January, February, and March, when it is open only Monday through Friday. Its twenty-two rooms contain much of the original furnishings, which are from the period from 1820 to 1860. All of the woodwork is woodgrained to resemble mahogany or rosewood. The house was decorated not long after the excavation of Pompeii, when mustard yellow, soldier blue, and Pompeii red were in vogue.

THE GAFFOS HOUSE

Portsmouth, Virginia

T he grizzled old sea captain didn't know when he had prayed last. It must have been many years ago, but it hadn't saved her. His lovely Maureen had died anyway. She had never been a strong one, and, when the baby was born and there were complications, she was gone in a day or two. But behind her she had left a treasure—tiny Cathy.

Fortunately, his mother had stepped in and taken care of the infant. It was hard to realize that Cathy was now a young girl. For the past two years, since his mother's passing, Cathy had made a home for him. Now he was close to losing her, too.

"God, don't let the girl die. I know I could have been a better man, and I don't deserve her. I never have talked much to you. Maybe I don't know how. But I'm trying, Lord." On he went, up the steps of the four-story house that had been turned into a hospital for Portsmouth's yellow-fever victims. The house was filled with patients, and beds had even been placed in the halls. Cathy was on the fourth floor, and that day she was tossing and turning so much that it made tears run down the old captain's weather-beaten cheeks just to watch her.

He cradled her frail body in his arms, pleading, "I will take you to Richmond and buy you such lovely clothes—everything you want. Look at me; speak to me! Cathy, you must get well, you must," he would cry out. But like many other poor souls who were brought to the hospital, turning and tossing in the throes of the virulent yellow fever, Cathy did not get well.

A Portsmouth gentleman who swears that his seagoing grandfather knew the captain says that the latter stayed out at sea as much as he could from then on. He was well–known on the busy waterfront, and, when he returned for brief shore stays, his solitary figure could be seen striding along in front of the homes a few blocks from the water. There he often paused to stare up at the fourth-floor windows of the house at 218 Glasgow Street.

How could so much happen in this cheerful-looking house? The house is yellow with blue shutters, and its interior is bright with shades of red, green, and gold. But the house did not always look this attractive. When Mary Alice and George Gaffos were first married, they moved into a ground-floor apartment here, as the old house was then divided into apartments. A full English-basement home, it is four stories above ground . The couple soon began to dream of buying and restoring it, despite its unhappy history and their modest income.

A few years later, however, they did buy and remodel it. Their dream had come true, but it was not all that they had expected. Or should we say that the house contained more than they expected and could ever have believed?

George and Mary Alice Gaffos are a pleasant, attractive couple. George attended Western Kentucky, and is now with B.F. Goodrich Company as District Manager for the State of Virginia. His family home is the house next door to 218 Glasgow. The Gaffos love Portsmouth and have both lived here since birth. Their two girls are no longer children. Andrea is attending Old Dominion University, and Sabrina is a third-grade teacher. They, too, could tell much about the house.

"From the first few weeks we lived here, strange things happened. The children noticed it first. Andrea would call us time after time, telling us she had heard heavy feet going up the stairs." The girls were on the third floor. Mary Alice remembers how frightened they were for a while. "One night Andrea called, and I ran up to her room. 'It was going up the stairs again tonight, Mother,' she said. 'I could hear the footsteps tramping up each tread, like someone with boots on, and I wonder if those feet are going to stop at the top of the stairs on my floor. I just hold my breath!'

"She threw her arms around my neck and hung on to me for dear life. Then the older girl chimed in. 'They never stop, though. They go right on up to the fourth floor, Mother, and sometimes we can hear them in one of the rooms overhead.'

"George and I got so frustrated for a while, we really didn't know how to handle it, for we thought the children were just hearing old-house noises. I made up all sorts of funny and comforting stories about the steps on the stairs to take their fear away. After a while, they said they weren't afraid anymore.

"One winter evening about a year later, my husband and I were sitting in front of the fire, working a puzzle. We enjoy doing them and sometimes sit up quite late. I remember that I had just found a piece we had been looking for all evening and was putting it in the right place when—Bam! The front door slammed so hard we both nearly jumped out of our chairs. We sat looking at one another, frozen for several seconds and waiting to see what would happen next.

"Then came a series of thuds that sounded like heavy boots going up the stairs, step by step. We heard them reach the top of the first floor. They went on. When they got to the third floor, George rose from his chair and looked out into the hall. I was terribly frightened. 'If they stop at the third floor, I'm going up there, Mary Alice,' he said. We stood there listening, and each step was so distinct. When the steps were almost at the third-floor landing, I wondered if the girls were awake and listening. I hoped not. The steps seemed to pause. Then we heard them again. Now, if it were a man, he was on his way up to the fourth floor.

"I was so relieved until we heard the door at the top of the stairs open and slam hard as it shut. I think I screamed, and George's face turned white as he ran out into the hall and up the stairs with me close behind him. We were very much afraid, and we both wondered what we were going to find in the room at the head of the stairs. At the third floor I stopped and switched on the light upstairs, but, when we reached the landing, no light at all could be seen under the door.

"'I'm not going into a completely dark room. Stay right here,' said George. 'I'll get the flashlight and be back in a second.' It seemed as if he were gone forever, but it probably wasn't over a minute or two until he returned. 'Get behind me,' he whispered, and I did. He threw open the door and swung the powerful flashlight from one end of the room to the other. The room was empty! With relief, we both just collapsed into each other's arms.

"Nothing happened for about a month after that. Then one night, when George was working on the third floor on something he had brought home from the office and I was reading to Sabrina, he called downstairs.

"'What are the girls doing playing in the attic this late?'

"'What do you mean?'

"'I hear them walking all over the place up there.'

"'You couldn't,' I said. 'Sabrina is down here with me, and Andrea is asleep in her bedroom up there with you.' I heard George go into Andrea's room, and in a few minutes he came downstairs, carrying the sleeping child in his arms.

"'I want you all to get out of the house immediately. There is someone upstairs. Go across the street, and, if you hear a gunshot, call the police.'

"He searched the attic, looked under beds, and opened closet doors on every floor of the house; but like the night the two of us went up to the attic, there was nothing to be found, at least nothing anyone could see.

"My mother, Mrs. Newton, probably had one of the strangest experiences of all. We were going on a business trip, and she volunteered to spend the night with the girls. She slept in our room, which

The front door of 218 Glasgow Street opens in the night, heavy footsteps can be heard going up three flights of stairs, and the attic door closes behind the ghost. This historic Virginia home is on the Old Portsmouth Halloween "Haunted House Tour" each year.

is right between the girls' bedrooms. Just as it does at home, her little dog slept on a pillow beside the bed. In the middle of the night, Mrs. Newton awoke to a thump, thump, thump. The first thing she thought about was the ghost. She determined that she wasn't frightened and that she was going to see if anything was there.

"Thinking it might be her dog, she said, 'Susie, now you get right back on the pillow.' She reached over to touch her and found the dog was there. Then mother Newton exclaimed out loud to herself, 'My Lord. It is the ghost!'

"Her finger flipped the light switch, and, when the light went on, she saw her bedroom slippers being tossed up into the air. Up and down and up and down. To her the bizarre and frightening spectacle seemed to last forever, but it was probably only a few seconds. She did not get to sleep until after the sun came up."

Mary Alice Gaffos and her family have lived at 218 Glasgow now for a quarter of a century. "Sometimes months go by and nothing happens. Then we may see our dog looking as if he is ready to spring into space and barking his head off as he faces an empty corner in the front hall. When that happens, we know the captain is back!"

If the daughter of the sea captain really did die in this house during the yellow-fever epidemic, it surely broke the old man's heart. Does his love for her still go on in some timeless dimension? Has it sometimes brought him back?

If you really want to visit the site of the haunting, The Gaffos House located at 218 Glasgow Street is one of the houses on the Old Portsmouth Ghost Tour. The tour takes place every year on the last Friday in October. Everyone meets first at Trinity Episcopal Church, for the cemetery is a fitting place to start.

HULL-HOUSE

Chicago, Illinois

It was a warm, humid July day as I stood on the planting strip in the middle of the busy Chicago street, looking at a large, two-story house, once the home of Jane Addams. Active in both her support of women's right to vote and an eight-hour workday for women and in her opposition to child labor, Mrs. Addams will always rank as an outstanding American.

As much traffic as I watched pass the front of it in the summer of 1985, it was hard to realize that, when this white frame house with its big front porch was built in 1856, it was a country home. Even if it were not for the bizarre story from the past that continues to be told about this place called Hull-House, I would still want to tour it because of my admiration for Jane Addams, who by 1910 was one of America's most popular women. She was the first American woman to win the Nobel Peace prize.

The Italianate house looks much as it did while she lived in it. The hand-carved molding around the doors and windows is unusually beautiful. Most of the furnishings and the artwork are original. A red-carpeted stairway leads up to the second floor. The first few years after she moved here in 1889, all of her activity centered on this house.

A picture of her hangs in the hall just outside the door of her second-floor office. Jane Addams is wearing a dark dress with a high neck and a white-lace dickey. She has a strong nose and mouth. Her eyes are straightforward and have a compassionate expression. There is also a tinge of humor about that face. Inside the office is her large desk with the brass oil lamp, old-fashioned telephone, and a magazine of the period appropriately titled *Work*.

While spending three months in Egypt and Syria, Jane Addams was impressed by the women filling their jars from the Nile, bearing them to the parched fields, and returning with scarcely enough to keep their children alive.

The upstairs bedroom on the left is the one people thought was occupied by the original "Rosemary's Baby." They often stood staring at these windows of Jane Addams's Hull-House.

Shortly after she came back to Chicago, she said, "These somber reflections may have prepared me for the visit of the Devil Baby at Hull-House, which occurred soon after our return. The knowledge of his existence burst upon the residents of Hull-House one day when three Italian women, with an excited rush through the door, demanded that the Devil Baby be shown to them. They knew exactly what he was like with his cloven hoofs, his pointed ears, and his diminutive tail. The Devil Baby had, moreover, been able to speak as soon as he was born and was most shockingly profane." (This quotation is taken from Addams's autobiographical *Twenty Years at Hull-House*.)

For six weeks, streams of visitors came to the house all day long and far into the night. One story held that a pious Italian girl was married to an atheist. Her husband in a rage had torn a holy picture from the bedroom wall, saying that he would quite as soon have a devil in the house as such a thing, whereupon the devil incarnated himself in her coming child.

Another version related that the father of six daughters had said, before the birth of a seventh child, that he would rather have a devil in the family than another girl, and the Devil Baby was the result of his careless, cruel words.

A more sinister version was that the father of the Devil Baby had married without first confessing a hideous crime committed years before, thus basely deceiving his innocent bride and the priest who performed the solemn ceremony. The sin had become flesh in his child, which, to the horror of the young mother, had been born with all the outward aspects of the devil himself.

As soon as the Devil Baby was born, he ran around the table shaking his finger at his father, who finally caught him and, in fear and trembling, brought him to Hull-House. When the residents there, in spite of the baby's shocking appearance, took him to church for baptism, in the wish to save his soul, they found that the shawl *was* empty, and the Devil Baby, fleeing from the holy water, was prancing over the back of the pews.

The vivid interest of so many old women in the story of the Devil Baby may support the theory that tragic experiences gradually become tales that prove of some use in the world. For it seems that this is a world that learns best through hardship and that the strivings and sufferings of those now dead are often transmuted into legendary wisdom. There is a warning in stories like this one.

Numbers of men came by, one group from a neighboring factory, and offered to pay to see the child, insisting it must be at Hull-House because "the women had seen it." To Jane Addams's question as to whether they supposed she would exhibit a poor, little, deformed baby if one had been born in the neighborhood, they replied, "Why not? It teaches a good lesson."

To many, this story of the child kept on the second floor of Hull-House, with its direct connection between cause and effect, between wrongdoing and punishment, brought soothing and relief. It restored confidence as to the righteousness of the universe.

Because the Devil Baby embodied an undeserved wrong to a poor mother whose tender child had been claimed by the forces of evil, hundreds of women came who had been humbled and disgraced by their children—mothers of the feeble-minded, of the vicious, of the criminal. They could speak out freely because, for once, a man responsible for an ill-begotten child had been "met up with" and had received his just deserts.

Perhaps the women were impelled by a longing to see one good case of retribution before they died, as a bullied child hopes to deal his tormentor at least one crushing blow when he "grows up."

Jane Addams left both her day nursery and her college courses for the underprivileged to listen to many tragic stories from the visiting women, stories of children maimed and burned because the mothers had no one to leave them with when they went to work and of beloved little bodies snatched by death because "he wouldn't let me send for the doctor," or "there was no money to pay for medicine."

The mother of a feeble-minded boy told such a story. "I didn't have a devil baby myself, but I bore a poor 'innocent' who made me

fight devils for twenty-three years." She told of other little boys who
had put him up to stealing and then had hidden in safety, leaving him
to be caught with the merchandise in his hands. "I've fought off bad
men and boys from the poor lamb with my very fists. Nobody ever
came near our house except such boys and the police officers who
were always arresting him."

It was as if the young mother of the grotesque Devil Baby, that
victim of wrongdoing on the part of another, had revealed to this
tragic woman much more clearly than soft words had ever done that
retribution for evil done to the innocent is sure. If she were destined to
walk all her life with the multitude who bear the undeserved wrongs
of the world, she would be walking in the companionship of others.

Although these events occurred more than seventy-five years
ago, it is difficult to tour the spacious, beautiful rooms of Hull-House
today without wondering about this story's validity. There are always
deformed children being born, and their plight was severe before the
days of plastic surgery, therapy, and the right these children now have
to special education.

Do we not know the temperament of Jane Addams well enough
to speculate that she may have rescued and sheltered such a child? She
would not have shown it under any circumstances, and only unequivo-
cal denial could have protected it from the curious.

Some say that the idea for the film *Rosemary's Baby* was derived
from the story of the Devil Baby at Hull-House. The house, which may
be toured today, was once called "the neighborhood center" by the
city's immigrants. For many of them it was the only place they could go
to find encouragement, receive help, and have a roof over their heads.

Today, looking up at the windows of the second floor, an old-
fashioned Victorian light fixture may be seen through the curtains of
the front room on the left. Did that light once shine down on a child
Jane Addams was too compassionate to allow the rest of the world to
see? Was the Devil Baby no more an offspring of the Devil than you or
I, but really a deformed child, and the name a result of superstition
and ignorance?

Will anyone ever know?

---

*Jane Addams's Hull-House, located at 800 South Halsted, Chicago, Illinois, is
open for tours. Telephone (312) 413-5353 for information about tours.*

HOUSES OF BEVERLY HILLS

Beverly Hills, California

Have you ever wanted to tour some of the movie-star homes that are said to be haunted? That is what we did last summer with a star-stuck young Britisher, Graham Hill, who owns his own tour company.

"Graham, I am not interested in just seeing homes where movie stars live, only the ones that have had ghost stories reported about them," I told him in advance so that he might plan our route.

Our first stop was 1005 North Rexford, Beverly Hills, just at the turn to Coldwater Canyon. I must admit that it did not look haunted, but then, neither do so many other places that are reputed to have ghosts. It was a gray stucco, multiterraced house with French doors and wrought-iron balconies that had once belonged to movie star Clifton Webb. An entrance set off by Corinthian columns gave the home the appearance of a Greek temple. While we were there, it was being remodeled. Workmen were repairing the molding above the columns, and scaffolding encircled the house.

Webb never married and seemed content to remain in the company of his mother, Maybelle. They were one of the most popular couples of the Hollywood social set and often entertained here. When Maybelle died in 1960, Webb kept her clothes and belongings in a locked room. He believed that the ghost of his mother and that of the popular actress and singing star Grace Moore were present in the house. Moore had lived in the house years before.

Owners of the home since Webb's death in 1966 have reported seeing his ghost. There is one room in particular in which a tall, misty apparition was said to walk back and forth repeating, "Well, well . . . ," over and over. After seeing this several times, the owners contacted close friends of Webb and discovered that this was one of the actor's favorite expressions. The owners insist that when they have had parties, they have often been questioned about the identity of a tall,

The privacy of "Pickfair" in Beverly Hills is protected by its large wrought-iron gate with cherubs on each column. There was already a ghost here when Douglas Fairbanks Sr. and Mary Pickford moved into the house.

distinguished-looking gray-haired man who guests described as "appearing to be someone very important."

The most unsettling experience occurred to a lady who was certain she saw the face of a man looking into the house from the courtyard outside. She described with astonishing exactitude the features of the late actor. The ghost is most often reported in October, the same month Clifton Webb died from a heart attack.

At Pickfair, 1143 Summit Drive, little of the house can be seen except the brick columns with cherubs on top on either side of the entrance. A video camera as well as the gate protect the occupants of the house from intrusion. The home belonged to one of the most popular couples in Hollywood history, Mary Pickford and Douglas Fairbanks Sr. Fairbanks purchased the site in 1918, and at that time all it contained was a small hunting lodge that they remodeled, turning it into a rambling, white-brick mansion. Pickfair, so dubbed by a reporter, had a hundred-foot-long swimming pool, the first in Beverly Hills. There are rumors that, when the Fairbanks moved in, this house already had a ghost and that a great tragedy had occurred here.

Late one night the couple was alone in the house, and Mary Pickford complained of hearing voices. Fairbanks began to tease her about it, but when they heard the sound of feminine footsteps, they hurried into the hall. Both of them saw the figure of a woman at the foot of the stairs carrying a sheet of music in her hand. As they stood there dumbfounded, she slowly ascended the first few stairs and then vanished.

Mary Pickford lived there until her death in 1979. In 1980 the forty-two-room mansion was purchased by sports entrepreneur Jerry Buss for $5.5 million, and it is said that his monthly payments are $350,000.

Falcon Lair, at 1436 Bella Drive, is the scene of another Hollywood haunting. this house was purchased for $175,000 in 1925 by that great romantic star of silent movies, Rudolph Valentino, for his wife, Natasha Rambova. He named the sixteen-room mansion Falcon Lair after a movie he was planning but never made. When his actress-wife left him soon thereafter, he moved in alone. He lived in the house for only a year before his tragic death from peritonitis at age thirty-one. His funeral, including a procession in which thousands participated across America, was accompanied by a massive outpouring of grief and an epidemic of hysteria and suicides. Spiritualists and mediums from all over the United States began to report receiving messages from Valentino from the next world.

Stories abound about this house, the former home of Rudolph Valentino.

Soon there were stories that the house was haunted. Realtors showing the property discounted these stories, but none of them could deny that strange, eerie noises were sometimes heard in the corridors and empty rooms. Some realtors, fearful of specters, refused even to show the property. While the house was up for sale, Standard Oil heiress Millicent Rogers rented it for three months. She left after only one night, later telling friends that she had been pursued down a lonely corridor by the ghost of Valentino.

The house was not easy to sell, not only because of the Depression but because the sale of a haunted house or of one reputed to be haunted sometimes offers problems. People who love haunted houses cannot always afford them.

Other famous people who have either lived in or rented Falcon Lair have been conductor Werner Janssen and his actress-wife, Ann Harding; Gloria Swanson, who rented it briefly; and absentee owner, North Carolina tobacco heiress Doris Duke.

It is a beautiful Spanish-style home draped with crimson bougainvillea. Occasionally, passersby report that they have stood and listened in astonishment to the music of the 1920s blaring forth from the house. And others say they have actually seen that idol of thousands of women, Valentino himself, dressed as a Spanish gaucho, striding through the courtyard in a striking costume of black and silver.

The darkly handsome Valentino was a man who never really believed that he could die like other men, and some think his flamboyant spirit still does not know its owner is dead.

During their marriage, Valentino and Rambova believed strongly in mediums and attracted this type of person to their home, so it is not surprising that many of Valentino's spiritualist friends claim they have communicated with his spirit. Reports of what he supposedly said, according to his widow, a medium, and a member of the American Society for Psychic Research, include Valentino's descriptions of heaven. And then there was controversy over the legitimacy of all this, which *Photoplay* magazine indicted as "Hollywood hokum," describing stars as lucrative victims for mediums.

Surely, few places see happenings more bizarre than do the homes of the stars. The George Reeves house at 1579 Benedict Canyon is one of them. After eight years of playing Superman on television, the forty-five-year-old Reeves was found dead on the floor of his bedroom in 1959. Reeves had been shot in the back of the head, and a gun was found on the floor between his legs. The coroner ruled that Reeves had committed suicide as the result of a waning career, but his mother claimed that it was murder, rather than suicide. She put the body on ice until she could prove that the wound was not self-inflicted.

Unsuccessful in proving this, Mrs. Reeves finally shipped her son's body back East for burial. Five years later, in 1964, she died, still claiming that he had been murdered. Friends who agreed with her have returned to this house over the years to hold séances in an attempt to contact his spirit and determine the identity of the killer. Owners of the home report that they were forced to move because of ghostly apparitions and incidents. This neighborhood has seen other violence, too: Only a few doors away is the house where the grisly Manson murders took place.

At 1018 Pamela Drive, we found the first private road that had no gate. At worst we could only be asked to leave. At best it was a path to adventure-inviting exploration. Facing the end of the drive was a beautiful white-stucco villa with a drift of brilliant red bougainvillea over the front door, palm trees on either side, and two Rolls-Royces parked in the front. It was one of the show places of the area. In the 1920s, when he moved from Muirfield to this Italian villa, Buster Keaton said that he used to think a house was a place to live but had found that it was something you moved from.

He was a complex person, one who often had difficulty separating the real from the unreal, the actor from his roles, the fact that you don't act life, you live it. Essentially, he was a comedian but one with a theme, man's duel with machines and circumstances. In the movie *Daydreams*, he flees the police in a chase scene by a broad jump to a ferry at the dock, only to realize the boat is coming in. He flees to the inside of the great, whirring paddle wheel trying desperately to keep

This Italian villa in Beverly Hills was formerly the home of stone-faced comedian Buster Keaton.

above water. He is dragged under, and then he is climbing up again. It is under again, up again, faster and faster, on a wheel that will turn forever.

The Keaton house is currently the home of actor Dick Christie, star of the former televison comedy *Small Wonder*. Christie is convinced that the ghost of Buster Keaton inhabits the house and says it plays eerie tricks on him and his family. They are tricks that often involve mechanical devices. "My wife, Chris, got up in the middle of the night to get some cough medicine and said, 'I can't find the light switch.' At that moment the hall light switched on. She left it on, and, as soon as she got back into bed, off went the light. We just lay there, certain someone was in the house and too scared to get up and look, until finally we went to sleep in spite of ourselves.

"One morning shortly after we moved in, I was expecting some important early morning phone calls. I woke up early, waiting for the calls to come. It grew later and later. When we tried to make a call out, the phone was dead. We tried another line, and it was dead, too. Then we discovered that both phones had been unplugged. The last thing we had done before we went to sleep the night before was to take an incoming phone call."

A prominent parapsychologist says there is little doubt but that the strange occurrences are caused by the ghost of Buster Keaton amusing himself. Playing with lights and unplugging phones would be completely in character for his ghost, says Dr. Erik Marten of the European Institute of Psychic Research.

Jean Harlow's home — Does the spirit of the actress still linger inside these walls?

Former home of the blond bombshell of the 1930s, Jean Harlow, where she and her husband, Paul Bern, were married in the living room.

In Westwood, 1353 Club View Drive is so hidden by trees that it is almost invisible from the street. This impressive two-story house was the home of actress Jean Harlow and her husband, Paul Bern, who committed suicide in 1932. This was the Harlow family home and her spirit is said to return to haunt the house.

Over at 2398 Laurel Canyon Boulevard in Hollywood Hills, the estate of the late magician Harry Houdini is a lonely, desolate place. The wind blows across weed-covered stairs, all that is left of the ruins of the house he built in the 1920s. Houdini's famous promise—if there were a way to return from the dead, he would do so—has echoed through the decades since his death. Ghostly happenings have been reported here, although no one is certain that it is the magician returning to haunt his estate. Friends who knew him well say that, if anyone in the world could escape the confines of the grave and come back, it would be the Great Houdini. They wait, convinced that somehow he will make himself known.

These homes have gates or sensor-alarm systems and are not open to the public. Readers who wish to view them must do so from the street.

WOODBURN

Dover, Delaware

When Governor Charles L. Terry of Delaware selected as a possible executive mansion an eighteenth-century Dover house, it appealed to him and his wife as a stately, serene old home. It was also one of the finest examples of Federal architecture in America. Woodburn was built in 1790 by John Hillyard on a tract given his great-grandfather by William Penn. The brick is a soft, mellow mauve; the windows are large, and the fanlight over the front door sparkles in the sunlight. It is surrounded by tall pines and trim English boxwoods. Terry certainly did not worry about the stories that the house was haunted. But there is at least one person who will never forget the apparitions of Woodburn.

In his seventies now, Albert Pennington Cooper is one of the craftsmen who have done restorative work on the 176-year-old mansion. On one October afternoon, when he and his helper, Troy, were almost ready to leave, a storm came up suddenly. "One moment we had plenty of light, but within the half hour it was as dark outside as if it was night. The wind was blowing so, and the branches waving, I thought some of those big trees were going to go. Then rain came down so hard and heavy that, for a while, it was pelting the house like buckshot.

"We didn't know whether a tornado was going by or just a bad storm. We would have been drenched if we had tried to make a run for the truck, so Troy and I sat down to wait for it to pass over. The next thing we knew we heard the sound of voices and shouting. Strong vibrations shook the whole house. You might have thought it was from the storm, and Troy and I looked at each other. I knew he didn't think that racket was wind or rain, and neither did I. It was like an angry undertone of people, and above it I heard a shriller sound, more like a woman's voice screaming than a man shouting.

"'Troy, I'm going to find out what's in that basement,' I said. I started down the stairs with my flashlight aimed ahead of me. Going

171

The Delaware Governor's House, known as "Woodburn," is also home to three recorded ghosts. Another interesting feature of the house is a basement tunnel that leads to the St. Jones River. It was once used by escaping slaves. (Governor's Office, Dover, Delaware.)

down I could hear the noise getting louder. Right behind me came Troy with a hammer in his hand. Whatever was down there, he was ready for it. At that moment the voices suddenly became quieter, and we began to hear the sound of hurrying footsteps from below.

"When we reached the basement it was brighter than I had expected. In fact, the hand holding my flashlight dropped to my side, for we didn't need it. What could be illuminating it so, I don't know. Have you ever seen cloud forms that resemble people? We all have, but not like these. I wondered if Troy saw them, too. 'What do you see, Troy?' I whispered, and I don't know why I whispered except that, all around me, everything was now dead silence. The forms were shifting and moving expressively, but, at the same time, they were more distinct than ever.

"'I see some people over at the end of the basement, and the way they move, they're scared, Al,' he replied. I saw them, too, but I wanted to hear what he thought. He said, 'They're all huddled up together, and I think some are crying.' There was a rattling noise and the sound of something being dragged along the floor.

"'Chains! Hear them?' asked Troy. Now the smoky forms seemed to mill about, pushing and shoving as if in panic. Then came a loud crash that actually hurt our ears, and it was real. You couldn't doubt that. It struck me as being like the noise of iron bars falling on the ground. It went on and on, the metallic ring traveling through the house with one clanking echo after another.

"Troy and I went up those basement stairs two at a time and slammed the door behind us. It didn't matter what kind of storm was going on, I was ready to leave. We gathered up our tools and were outside before you could say Jackie Robinson! Do you know, the storm had stopped and the sun was setting clear.

"'That last crash was enough to wake the dead wasn't it, Troy?' I asked.

"He took me by the arm, and those big eyes of his wore the strangest look I'd ever seen in them as he said, 'Al, what do you mean, wake the dead? Those were the dead.'

"Well, that really gave me the creeps. Every Sunday, regular as clockwork, my wife and I are at St. Paul's Methodist, and the Bible verse that came to my mind suddenly was 'If a man die, shall he live again?' I asked Troy, 'Were they dead or alive?'

"'Man, I don't know. We can't go where they are, 'cause that's a notch up the ladder. But they sure can get back here.' And with that, he drove off in his old battered blue pickup. Now, Troy was just a helper. He didn't have a bunch of degrees and such, but I always envied him for what he did have, kind of a special way of talking to the Lord and getting answers.

"That was on a Friday, and I didn't need Troy there at the house again until I was finished with some of my own work. That would probably be a couple of weeks, so Monday I was back alone. I spent the entire morning on the job listening to every sound, just waiting for something to happen, but nothing did. All that week Woodburn was just as peaceful and quiet as you please, and I was beginning to think that the storm had given me a super case of the jitters.

"The second week, it seemed to me the house was extra quiet. Sometimes, in these places a hundred or more years old, you get used to the various, ominous creaks and the sound of the wind exploring the crevices. After a week or two, it's as if the house is talking under its breath. Maybe it's talking to itself or to the folks who once lived there, but not to you. So you don't pay it any mind.

"On Thursday night I had to go out and have myself a little fun, and I stayed up way too late. I was on the job at Woodburn by seven-thirty next morning, but by midafternoon I was really dragging. There was one more task that I needed to do in the house that day, but it would take close attention to do it just right. Since I had priced the work at Woodburn by the job, if I wanted to take a thirty- or forty-minute nap, it was nobody's business but mine. I folded up a jacket I kept there for a pillow, pulled my coat up over me, and was soon fast asleep.

"At three-thirty, I was awakened by a noise that would murder sleep for anyone. I heard a tremendous crash that went rolling and reverberating through the house, apparently coming from the lower level. I got up and looked out the window, and it was a gray day but with no storm in sight. Then there came a terrible series of rattling and banging that shook the entire room. I could tell all of this was coming from inside the house. If it had been anywhere but Dover, I would have thought I was in an earthquake.

"It reminded me of the afternoon when Troy had been here during the storm, so I made up my mind to go to the basement. I had no sooner gotten down there than I was aware of smoke, but there was no fire to be seen, and the smoke didn't smell as if wood was burning or like oily rags.

"For the first minute or so I couldn't see a thing, but when I did, there were the figures like Troy and I had seen before. Only this time three were much clearer than the rest. It appeared to be a woman and two men, and one of them was coming after her. I saw the other man lift up his hands and drop what seemed to be a large, fat coil of smoke down over his head. When he did, there were the most terrible sounds I ever heard, for the man's screams merged with eerie cries of glee from the other figures. A loud, thunderous crash sounded again, and there were such strong vibrations, they went right through me. I don't know what happened after that.

"When I came to, I was lying on the floor in the upstairs hall, a few feet from the basement door. I went into the big living room, and there was some light coming in the big windows and making a path across the floor. It was night by now, but there was a moon. There was also something else, and it was in the house with me. Right now, it was coming up from the basement, and, as it came, there was a muffled, clanking sound on each step. I heard it stop in front of the door to the stairs. But the door never opened. Instead, I saw a dark shadow on the door, and the outline of a man's figure began to emerge. Gradually, it came on through, and there, a few feet from me, stood the apparition.

"I think I gasped and stepped back, but he never once looked my way. He was not so distinct that I could tell anything about the color of his clothes, but he was distinct enough for me to know him for a man. I began to think of the stories about Woodburn, stories of a secret tunnel that connects this house with the St. Jones River behind it, stories of when Woodburn belonged to a Quaker named Daniel Cowgill and was a busy stop on the Underground Railway. In the years before the Civil War, runaway slaves from Maryland and all over the South were sheltered here until Cowgill could help them on their way to Canada or a free state. Sometimes the slave catchers would raid the house and take runaways back by force.

"I'm ashamed now that I didn't take off after that strange figure as I watched it head toward the front door, but I didn't. I sat down on the floor with my back to the wall, and my hand shook so, it took me three tries to light up a cigarette and calm down some. "If I remembered the story rightly, I didn't want to follow the apparition or even go out to my van, for, if I did, I would have to walk right past its destination. If the specter was the slave kidnapper who had met his end here, he was headed straight for the hanging tree. There is no way I wanted to see a body hanging from that gnarled, old tulip poplar out there in the yard, the tree with the hook imbedded in its hollow.

"Either I passed out or went to sleep briefly, but, when I next looked out the window, the moon was high in the sky. I had to get out of here. As I hurried toward my van, the gusts of wind were like strong fingers flinging wet leaves through the air and sometimes in my face. I didn't turn my head. Then I recalled my tools. Should I leave them until next morning or go back to the house and get them? I turned around, and, when I did, my eyes were inevitably drawn toward the big poplar and to the hollow in its trunk.

"There was the sight I had dreaded to see! In the moonlight hung the struggling body of a man, twisting and turning, this way and that, suspended by a rope from the hook in the old hanging tree. If a man dies, will he live again? I turned and ran to the van. On the way home it was hard for me to think, I was so frightened. Why should I hear and see all that? My great-grandfather Pennington was a slave in Maryland, and he ran away from his master. He went through Delaware on his way North, maybe even to Dover. But what did that have to do with me? If a man dies, will he live again?"

This is one of several ghost stories in connection with Woodburn, the governor's house at 151 King's Highway, Dover, Delaware. In it there is also a colonial gentleman, a ghost who is a wine bibber, and a little girl in a red-and-white-checked gingham dress. For tour information, call (302) 736-5656.

ASHTON VILLA

Galveston, Texas

James Brown of Galveston was a proud man. He was proud of the fortune he had made in the hardware business, of building the first brick house in the state, of his lovely, golden-haired daughter Bettie, and of being a Texan.

It was fortunate that the palatial Ashton Villa was finished in 1859, for, due to the Civil War, nothing was built from 1861 to 1865. Galveston was blockaded during the greater part of the war, first captured by the Federals in October of 1862 and then recaptured three months later by the Confederates.

Born in 1855, "Miss Bettie," a lovely, golden-haired little girl, spent her childhood in an exciting atmosphere. During the war years the house served as a hospital for Confederate soldiers, and, as Galveston was alternately in the hands of both armies, Union and Confederate generals came and went, as it was a headquarters for both. Over and over again it has been said in Galveston that the swords of surrender were exchanged between the North and South in the Gold Room, Ashton Villa's ornate, formal living room.

Soon after the war, Galveston began to regain its prosperity. Wharves were again crowded with ships laden with merchandise, old stores were remodeled, and new ones were opened. Wartime damage was repaired, and returning soldiers came home to resume their trades and professions. It was a bustling port.

The late 1800s arrived and, with them, the island's glory days, when ships from around the world dropped anchor in Galveston's busy harbor. Fortunes were made overnight, and The Strand, business district of this seaside city, became the "Wall Street of the Southwest."

Galveston was one of the most picturesque and romantic cities in the South and a perfect setting for a beautiful woman. Here Rebecca Ashton Brown, favorite daughter of financier James M. Brown, lived an adventurous life, the likes of which most Victorian ladies did not even dare imagine. A legend in her own time, she scandalized

Miss Bettie was a free spirit. So free, there are some who believe that even after death she was able to return to beautiful Ashton Villa. (Photo courtesy Ashton Villa Historical Association.)

many with her liberated ways. She often traveled alone, smoked in public, and never married. This was shocking for a woman of her day.

"Miss Bettie," as she was most often known, was the epitome of the frivolity and opulence that the period exuded. A free spirit, she traveled to Munich, Düsseldorf, and other art centers of Europe. Preferring travel and adventure to giving up her freedom, she rejected marriage but had many beaux. One of them even quaffed champagne from "Miss Bettie's" gilded slipper.

Nine years after the Civil War, a fashionable summer resort for the wealthy opened in Waukesha, Wisconsin. It was called Fountain Spring House, and the arrival at its doors of a southern belle from Galveston, Texas, was reported in the *Milwaukee Journal*. "She made her appearance with sixteen trunks filled with such finery as Waukesha never before beheld on one woman; and with her carriage, her livery men, servants, a coachman, and coal-black horses." The other guests at the hotel were stunned by such a display.

Her beauty was emphasized by her magnificent gowns, and it was said that Miss Bettie often appeared in three different costumes in one day. It was always she who led the grand marches; and at one Christmas ball, she wore a handsome, black-velvet princess gown. On its train were fall leaves embossed in solid gold, and in her hand she carried an enormous ostrich fan studded with real pearls. That night her golden-haired Grecian beauty was a striking contrast to the appearance of her escort, an arrestingly handsome man with black hair and a beard. It was one of the few nights when Miss Bettie seemed to laugh delightedly and talk attentively with her escort.

From Galveston, she often traveled abroad, and these trips were an occasion to collect art objects and curios, paintings and tapestries from many foreign lands. Among her favorites were costumes from several countries, and a collection of unusual fans. All of these treasures were kept in a small alcove in the ornate living room called the Gold Room, where she often entertained until her death in 1920.

The old mansion itself has now become a museum. The atmosphere of the house has been beautifully restored with Miss Bettie's paintings, and her furniture. The Gold Room is almost as beautiful a showplace today as it was when she was alive.

The villa's carriage house has often been used as living quarters for a caretaker, and this is where Terry O'Donohoe stayed one weekend to help out a friend named Don Ross, the tall, darkly handsome young man who was caretaker of the mansion. Illness in the family necessitated Don's being away overnight, and, nothing being said to anyone, his friend simply took his place. It is doubtful if anyone even knew O'Donohoe was not the regular caretaker.

Just before O'Donohoe went to bed, he noticed some heat lightning and that the air outside was so still, not a leaf was stirring. We are going to get some rain, he thought. Buffy, Don's dog, was behaving peculiarly, following him everywhere and underfoot constantly. What was wrong with the animal? Perhaps Don was used to this, but it was getting on Terry's nerves. He decided to put the dog outside.

Sometime after midnight, Terry was awakened by an ear-shattering crash of thunder followed by smaller volleys close by. The dog was barking wildly. Terry's first thought was that someone was trying to break into the mansion, and, mindful of his duty, he hurriedly threw on his clothes. Outdoors the rain lashed at him angrily, and the sky was illuminated by one bolt of lightning after another. It was certainly the devil of a night. He ran under the eerie canopy of huddled trees near the villa, but nothing was any protection against the storm, and he was drenched.

Back inside, his first impression was that the house could not have been any quieter. He had turned on the lights and already checked two rooms, however, when he heard the sound of voices. It was a man and woman, and their voices were raised in angry argument. Shrinking back against the wall, he had almost decided that someone with a right to be in the house had come back unexpectedly when he realized that all was again silent.

He waited for about five minutes; then, still enveloped in that silence, he decided to continue his check of the house. When he reached the Gold Room, he was certain he heard a rustling sound coming from within the room, but what could it be? His fingers found the light switch just inside the door, and for a moment the room was ablaze with light. To his astonishment, he saw a woman seated at the piano and a man looking down at her. He flipped the switch off instantly.

He was certain the pair must have seen him, and at any moment he expected them to come after him. How could he explain who he was and what he was doing there at one o'clock in the morning? On the other hand, what were they doing there in the darkness? But even as he wondered, he had a strange feeling, a feeling that they belonged there and he did not. Moonlight was streaming in the windows, and his eyes soon adjusted to it. He watched the woman. What a beauty she was, with that golden hair piled on top of her head. She put a handkerchief up to her eyes and seemed to be crying. The tall man with dark, curly hair and a beard was trying to talk to her. Suddenly, it was as if a dial had been turned up on a radio, for he could hear their conversation as clearly as if they were right beside him.

"Bettie, do you know who Narcissus fell in love with when he looked in the pool?"

"He fell in love with his own beauty. But what are you trying to say?"

"It is foolish for any man to talk to you about marriage. You are like Narcissus. You couldn't really love anyone, for you are too absorbed in your own pleasures, your collecting of meaningless objects, and, most of all, your looks."

"Harrison, do you really believe what you are saying about me?"

"You are a real beauty, but I've come to know you too well, Bettie."

"I won't listen to this. You are hateful!" And with her chin stubbornly tilted upward and eyes straight ahead, she began playing the piano.

The man paced back and forth for a few minutes with an angry look on his face, and then Terry heard a creaking sound in the hall behind him and looked back. When his eyes returned to the scene in the Gold Room, the tall, dark-haired man was gone. The music stopped. The girl rested her head on her arms on the piano, and Terry knew she was crying.

He was about to leave as quietly as possible when the lady wiped her eyes, arose from the piano bench, and looked in his direction. For a moment he almost panicked and ran, for he thought a sound had betrayed him. She walked over toward some shelves filled with art objects. What an unusual dress she was wearing, but how it became her. It must be a costume out of the 1800s. Now she was not far from where Terry was concealed behind a Chinese screen. Standing in front of the shelves with her back to him, she reached up with her right hand and, taking something off the shelf, held it in front of her. What in heaven's name was she looking at? Then she turned around, and once more he was struck by her beauty. But what was it she was holding?

And then, he saw that she had an exquisite fan in her hands.

"Mirror, mirror on the wall. Who is the fairest one of all . . . ." she began in low, melodic tones as she held the fan beside her own lovely face and stared into the mirror. Then the fan fell from her hand.

Even as he looked at her, her lovely face seemed to fade and begin to disappear. Then she was gone. By morning it seemed more like a dream. His friend, Ross, returned early and stopped by the villa for a few minutes. When Ross came over to the carriage house, he was filled with excitement.

"Terry, you won't be able to believe it, but early this morning a valuable fan was taken from Miss Bettie's collection, and it was found on the floor. Can you imagine that?"

"No."

"Someone must have a strange sense of humor."

"I suppose so."

"The cleaning lady found it when she was vacuuming this morning. Didn't you hear her call?"

"No. I didn't hear a thing."

"Terry, why do you have such a strange expression on your face. You look as if you aren't telling me everything. If something happened last night over at the villa, you need to say so because I'm responsible."

"Responsible?"

"Yes, responsible. I'm responsible for 'Miss Bettie's house.' Now tell me what happened."

Terry told him how he had woken up at about one o'clock, when he heard the storm and the dog barking and thought someone was breaking into the mansion, and how, still not sure but that it might be burglars, he had cautiously entered the house and seen the couple in the Gold Room. When he got to the part about Miss Bettie carrying the fan over to the mirror, his voice began to tremble, and he was clearly upset. Ross was greatly interested.

"What did you think of her? Isn't she gorgeous? How did she look when you saw her last night?"

"Golden hair on top of her head, tall, great figure."

"She's a real beauty, all right. There is not a woman who can match Miss Bettie.

There isn't any way I would check on that house again at night. It's haunted, Don, and by more than one ghost. There was a man, dark, handsome . . ."

Ross interrupted. "And did she seem to care for him?"

"Great heavens, man. How should I know? We're talking about a ghost, don't you understand?

But Don Ross didn't really seem to be listening. He was examining his face intently in the mirror. Then he searched the dark, curly hair and beard for gray. "How strange he is," thought Terry as he watched him. He had just met Ross a few weeks ago. Maybe after he had known him longer . . . but Terry wasn't really sure he wanted to.

"I don't think we need to mention anything about your experience in the Villa. It will be our secret," Ross said as Terry left. Then he looked at his watch. It was one o'clock in the afternoon and he was already eager for the time to pass. He knew, if the dog barked, he would go. Suppose she was only a vision. She was the most romantic looking woman he had ever seen.

Ashton Villa and nearby historic buildings attract tourists the year around. For more information, write to Ashton Villa, Galveston Historical Foundation, 2328 Broadway, Galveston, TX 77550. Historic preservation, along with the beauty of the Gulf Coast, has made Galveston as glamorous a place today as it was in the late 1800s.